S0-BCS-284

TRUE
GRIZZ

true grizz

Glimpses of Fernie, Stahr, Easy, Dakota,
and Other Real Bears in the Modern World

DOUGLAS H. CHADWICK

SIERRA CLUB BOOKS
San Francisco

Text copyright © 2003 by Douglas H. Chadwick

Published by Sierra Club Books
85 Second Street, San Francisco, CA 94105
www.sierraclub.org/books

Produced and distributed by
University of California Press
Berkeley and Los Angeles, California
University of California Press, Ltd.
London, England
www.ucpress.edu

Book and jacket design by Elizabeth Watson
Photographs © Derek Reich, except Stahr and cub by garage, by Kai-Eerik Nyholm, which is
    © Wind River Bear Institute
Maps by Gray Mouse Graphics

"Right in the Trail," from *No Nature,* by Gary Snyder, © 1992 by Gary Snyder. Used by permission of Pantheon Books, a division of Random House, Inc.

Library of Congress Cataloging-in-Publication Data
Chadwick, Douglas H.
    True grizz : glimpses of Fernie, Stahr, Easy, Dakota, and other real bears
in the modern world / by Douglas H. Chadwick.
        p. cm.
    ISBN 1-57805-100-2 (hardcover : alk. paper)
        1. Grizzly bear—Behavior—Montana. 2. Wildlife management—Montana. I. Title
QL737.C27C44 2003
599.784'09786—dc21
                                                                                    2003042819

Printed in the United States of America on acid-free paper containing a minimum of
60% recovered waste, of which at least 30% of the fiber content is post-consumer waste

First Edition

07 06 05 04 03

10 9 8 7 6 5 4 3 2 1

For Russell Chadwick,

who has a way with small cats

and big bears

- - -

ACKNOWLEDGMENTS Several generous people reviewed drafts of the book, correcting factual errors and offering suggestions. The first three are Teal Chadwick, my daughter; Karen Reeves, my wife; and Elise Chadwick, my mother. This was not the first time Mom, age eighty-one, had perceived some need for improvement on the part of the author. Next come Paul Zalis, host of a literary program on National Public Radio; Barbara Lemmick, a wonderful artist; Derek Reich, photographer and filmmaker; Tim Manley, a bear conflict manager for the Montana Department of Fish, Wildlife & Parks; and Jim Williams, regional supervisor for that agency. I especially appreciate Mr. Williams's perseverance in light of the fact that the practice of giving wild animals names drives him half crazy and he had to put up with it from the subtitle on. Thank you kindly, each and all. And thank you, Doug and Lynne Seus, longtime friends, owners of Wasatch Rocky Mountain Wildlife, amazing bear trainers and dedicated conservationists, for opening my eyes to unguessed dimensions of grizz.

CONTENTS

PROLOGUE

However you come at the subject, truth about the nature of grizzlies is difficult to perceive. The last place you're likely to find much of it has been in accounts presented as true grizz tales. I'd like to try to change that.

Most grizzly stories are not really about grizzlies. They are about how people thought and felt and acted around the big bears. This book focuses on individual animals that I followed season by season, year after year, gathering details about their lives. In a sense, they told their own stories. I'm just passing them along, highlighting situations that brought unexpected dimensions of grizzly ecology, grizzly power, or grizzly intelligence into play.

Not that the pages to come aren't populated by humans. Local folks, tourists, bear fearers, and bear lovers all put in appearances. A couple of inspired wildlife specialists working to alter some of the ways humans relate to grizz—and, surprisingly, some of the ways grizz relate to us—have major roles in the tales that unfold. But my goal is the same from start to finish: to move beyond the ground mist of fables that envelops great bears, sidestep the images that turn out to be reflections of our own complicated nature, and keep on looking from fresh angles until we finally just see real grizzlies in the real world. They are fantastic enough.

- - -

Some quick background: I have a master's degree in wildlife biology. I earned it studying mountain goats among the peaks of northwestern

Montana's Swan Range from 1971 through 1974. At that time, these snow-white climbers were undergoing broad declines. The chief causes turned out to be liberal hunting quotas combined with the rapid spread of roads into former backcountry, mostly for logging. Grizzlies south of Canada were on an even sharper downward trend. Suspecting the same factors at work, I added a survey of the bears to my other fieldwork, comparing signs and sightings from roaded and roadless areas.

My efforts eventually played a minor role in establishing more conservative harvests of the goats and in adding grizzlies to the federal list of threatened species in the lower forty-eight states. Meanwhile, I moved north along the Great Divide and spent the next three years as a seasonal biologist in Glacier National Park, collecting more mountain goat data—and coming upon a lot more grizz. I then turned from writing scientific papers to freelance writing about natural history. I've been doing that for a quarter of a century now, circling the globe to cover creatures from elephants to jaguars to beetles on land, and from blue whales to corals in the saltwater realm. Yet the subject that I return to most often is the life of the grizzly bear.

This mammal is nothing if not solidly built to contend with whatever forces nature sends its way. But its future amid a fast-moving, fast-growing, technologically advanced society is parlous. Grizzly bear survival now depends less upon the biological traits that the species possesses—its evolutionary fitness—than upon how we think about grizz and what we do with their homelands as a result. Everything comes down to human perceptions. And yet seeing the bear for what it truly is, rather than what we hope or fear or unconsciously need a great silvertipped beast to be, remains a nearly insurmountable challenge.

On top of that, there is the uncertainty principle. In subatomic physics, it cautions that the act of measuring a particle affects the very properties being measured. Applied to grizz, it means that even objective accounts of supposedly normal bear behavior may in fact be descriptions of a bear reacting to the presence of the observer or other humans. This goes beyond obvious examples such as a silvertip lumbering about on two legs. As often as not, grizzlies portrayed as generally restless, wily, irritable, moody, or the like—*unpredictable* is a favorite term—are acting that way specifically because they know that someone is in the area. A bear may feel pressed, challenged, or possibly stalked, whether the person is armed with lethal firepower or only well-intentioned curiosity, and no matter how certain he is that the bear couldn't possibly have detected him.

To witness typical activities and emotions, the only method I know of is to sit patiently on a faraway hillside with a telescope. You'll need a stiff wind in your face too. Otherwise, given the unexcelled capabilities of this species' nose, you can't be sure that a bear won't pick up your scent from a stray gust.

Watch clear-eyed for long enough and you will find that every grizzly is unique, not just physically but also in terms of temperament, learning abilities, social status, and experience. If you do spend that kind of time, you are also likely to discover that, even when you do everything right, life in big bear country has a way of getting exciting far too fast. And during those moments, you learn more than a little about the nature of your own true self.

VITALS

Common Name: Grizzly bear.

Also Known as: Silvertip, *oso plateado* (Spanish for "silver-coated bear"), Bear That Walks Like a Man, Old Ephraim.

Names of Some Local Forms: Golden bear (California, gone by the 1920s), yellow bear (Mackenzie region, Canada), Toklat grizzly (interior Alaska; light gold coat with chocolate feet), brownie/big brown bear (coastal British Columbia and Alaska), Kodiak (Kodiak Island, Alaska).

Scientific Name: *Ursus arctos horribilis.* The species *Ursus arctos,* called the brown bear, is distributed around the Northern Hemisphere. Eurasian populations occur from Scandinavia to Russia's Pacific shores and as far south as northern India, Iran, and Spain. North America has a variety of identifiable races and ecotypes. Most experts classify them together as the subspecies *horribilis.* This includes the big bears of Kodiak Island and brown bears of the Pacific mainland coast, as well as the interior brown bears whose fur more often has the frosted, or grizzled, appearance that gave rise to the label *grizzly.* It is a common and accepted practice to refer to all New World brown bears as grizzlies.

General Characteristics: Large size; wide, dished face; prominent muscular hump above the shoulders; long, whitish, slightly curved claws. These traits distinguish grizzlies from the far more common North American species, *Ursus americanus,* which is smaller, with a narrower head and much shorter, more strongly curved claws. Though known as the black bear, it comes in brown, cinnamon, gold, bluish, and even white color phases as well.

Adult Weight: From 250 pounds (smallish females, Rocky Mountains) to 1,800 pounds (exceptional males, Alaska Peninsula and Kodiak Island).

Adult Length: 6 to 9 feet.

Adult Height at Shoulder: 3 to 4 feet.

Claw Length: 3.5 to 4 inches.

Top Speed: 30 to 35 miles per hour, with rapid acceleration.

Age at First Breeding: 3 or 4; 5 in marginal habitat.

Breeding Season: May or June; early July in the far northern range.

Birthing Season: January or early February. As in the weasel (or mustelid) family, reproduction in grizzlies involves delayed implantation. The embryo ceases development soon after conception and remains dormant until about November, when it becomes implanted in the wall of the uterus and resumes growing. Birth takes place two months later in the female's winter den, a dark, protected—womblike—environment, for continued early development.

Birth Weight: Just 1 to 1.5 pounds. The infant is nearly hairless, and its eyes remain closed for the first 10 days or longer.

Litter Size: 2 to 4. Twins are typical, triplets not uncommon, quadruplets somewhat rare.

Duration of Mother-Cub Association: 1 to 4 years; 2 or 3 years is usual.

Interval between Births: 2 to 4 years; most often 3.

Longevity: 25 to 30 years. One wild female in Montana, whose age was confirmed by counting annual tooth cementum layers, lived to be at least 35.

Intelligence: Keen, with rapid learning and strong long-term memory.

Emotions: Highly developed, varied, and potent.

Sociability: Semisolitary. Apart from the mother-young bond, associations are mostly transient, related to courtship and sharing of concentrated food supplies such as spawning salmon.

Typical Home Range (in square miles):		
	Females	Males
North Pacific Coast	<50	<100
Rocky Mountains	50-300	200-500
Arctic Barrengrounds	500+	800+

Original Numbers and Distribution: Unknown. Perhaps as many as 250,000 lived in the western half of the continent, with 50,000 to 100,000 of these south of Canada.

Current Numbers and Distribution: Alaska holds 20,000 to 35,000, and
Canada 20,000 to 30,000. The lower forty-eight states have roughly
1,000 to 1,300 distributed among 5 separate locales:

1. Greater Yellowstone Ecosystem (the Yellowstone National Park
   area of northern Wyoming, southern Montana, and eastern Idaho):
   400 to 600 animals, possibly more;
2. Northern Continental Divide Ecosystem (the Glacier National Park
   area of Montana): 400 to 600 animals;
3. Cabinet-Yaak Ecosystem (northwestern Montana): 10 to 35 animals;
4. Selkirk Ecosystem (northernmost Idaho): 25 to 40 animals on the
   U.S. side of the international boundary; and
5. North Cascades Ecosystem (northern Washington): 0 to 10 animals.

Reliable counts have been difficult to obtain, and thus estimates remain
open to dispute.

Status: Listed since 1975 as threatened in the Lower 48 under the
Endangered Species Act.

Bottom Line: Reliable information about the natural history of the grizzly
was unavailable before the brothers John and Frank Craighead carried
out their ground-breaking studies in Yellowstone National Park. They
didn't start until 1959, more than a century and a half after this giant
carnivore was first reported by white explorers. With help from technol-
ogy such as satellite monitoring and DNA analysis, new information is
being compiled far more quickly today. But scientists have a great deal
left to learn about one of the most complex mammals in existence, and
the public's conception is still based largely on old-fashioned, hair-rais-
ing yarns.

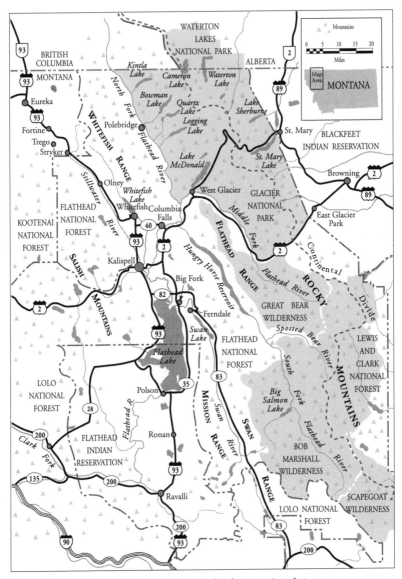

*The Flathead Region and Adjoining Lands in
the Northern Continental Divide Ecosystem*

SEEING THE BEAR

WHILE WORKING FOR a large mining company, my father, a geologist, found a promising lode of copper and molybdenum ore near Alaska's Kobuk River. He spent several field seasons exploring the site further, sampling strata with drilling rigs, sounding the stone depths of the world. I went with him for a summer. One afternoon, we were in a muddy patch where men and machines were stripping the taiga hide off the permafrost, when it was decided that I would hike back to camp. By myself. I don't know why. I was nine years old. My memory from that time is like a sketch pad left out in the weather.

Camp couldn't have been far. This was my first trip to the Arctic, though, and I had not yet been alone in that northern bush. After shoving through willows and black spruce a while, I began to worry about getting lost. That's probably what brought grizzlies to mind— that and all the talk about the big bears I had absorbed from guys on the project. They had shot a couple at the fringes of camp. I can remember one man hanging out bacon to lure more animals in, but, again, details elude me.

It wasn't long after I went on the alert for grizzlies during my hike that one appeared. Its bulk seemed to arise out of nowhere, and it panicked me into leaping across a stream. I didn't make the opposite bank. The current swept me along a short distance before I pulled myself out. I ran until I hit camp, soaking wet and insisting, as I would all summer, that I really had run into a bear. More likely, it was a clump of vegetation.

My father died some time ago. I never got around to asking him what he thought happened. My ability to recall those days dissolves by the year. And yet if I take out a pair of old leather work gloves impregnated with a certain brand of insect repellent and slowly inhale, I still see with utter clarity the stream setting and the gray color of the water I swam, just as I can make out the low rise that Dad and I climbed together after he woke me in the middle of the night for my first look at the northern lights.

The second time I saw a bear while afoot, there were three of us: myself, another preteen boy, and his younger sister. We were walking along a road through cutover woodland in northern Idaho not far from their lakeside summer home. As dusk fell, we started whispering about bears and shying at the dark stumps that converged on all sides. Before long, we had regressed nearly to the state of little children negotiating with monsters in the closet, afraid to breathe too loudly lest it set them amok.

I tried what I thought of as a grown-up trick, checking out suspect stumps by staring at them indirectly. In hopes of being a mountain man or explorer one day, I'd collected the fact that bush-savvy types rely on the corners of their eyes to pick up movement in poor light. And I knew why because I aspired to be a scientist too: the pupil's light and dark receptors are more densely packed toward the edges than in the center, which is largely given over to color receptors. What I hadn't learned is how everything begins to pulse and writhe when you stare at it long enough all keyed up and half in love with the possibility of being scared out of your wits.

From the adventure books and sportsmen's magazines heaped in my room, I'd gathered that people in the woods were always having ripsnorting run-ins with grizzly bears. For hardcore outdoorsmen, it was practically an obligation. If there were such things as average-size grizzlies, I'd never read about any, only about awesome grizzlies—that was the stock term—weighing at least half a ton. A tower of gut-crunching terror every time. With red eyes that glowed like embers. Crazed with bloodlust. Slavering foamy spit. I figured some of this was what Dad would call happy horseshit, but a lot of it must be true. How else could so many adults wind up with the same stories of humongous, berserker bears? Besides, I didn't have much else to go on.

While I forget who broke and ran first, I know that the other boy and I were a long way ahead of his little sister before we looked at each other and started to slow down. Finally, we decided that maybe we ought to stop and wait for her, in case . . . We felt ashamed but not very, having no idea what we could do to stop a bear from shredding a kid, anyway. This time, though, I never insisted later that there really had been a bear. None of us did. We just told our parents what we might have seen. If it was a bear, they said, it would have been a black bear, because grizzlies were gone from that part of the state. Well, the thing did look pretty dark, we agreed.

My first encounter with a flesh-and-blood grizzly came a decade or so later in the Swan Range of Montana's Rocky Mountains, one big valley north of the Bob Marshall Wilderness. My dreams of becoming an explorer and a scientist were fairly intact. I was beginning my graduate research on mountain goats in a remote jumble of high country, and I planned to stay among the herds on its cliffs year-round.

Reconnoitering the study area, I climbed toward an alpine ridge top for an overview. I was about to break above tree line when I saw a stout bear with a wide, dished face, a mound of muscle stockpiled above its shoulders, and coruscating, silver-tinged fur striding in my direction across an open slope. Fast. I had a hiking partner. She was also my research partner and my first wife. I shouted to her that we needed to get up a tree. After racing to a nearby subalpine fir, I was looking for handholds to pull myself higher when I realized that my wife was still on the ground behind me. Dammit! I was doing it again.

About that time, I also realized that the bear was still almost a quarter mile off. I could have sworn that it had been about to close in on us. My wife proceeded to climb another tree, but not before looking over at me with confusion and, as I remember it, disappointment in her eyes. We lost track of the grizzly and eventually worked our way back to the base of some cliffs to observe the resident goat herd through what felt like the dregs of the day.

I got braver. I had to. It was that or go home. Our main campsite was a tramped-out nook at the edge of a sheltering spruce grove. The cook-fire pit looked out upon the brushy lower slope of an avalanche track, which fanned onto the bank of a talkative, trouty creek. Both black bears and grizzlies frequented the slide area and traveled the streamsides. To hike a game trail that didn't include fresh bear tracks and droppings was unusual. Trees along the paths bore rubbed patches and claw marks, thought to serve the bears as signposts, and the pitch that oozed from the wounded bark held samplings of their hairs. Grizzly diggings cratered the high, open slopes. Grizzly daybeds pressed down wildflowers in the lee of ridgelines. There was no place I could go and avoid bears. I saw them around. I grew accustomed.

One particular glimpse early in the project put a different tint on those that came later. On a summer afternoon with nothing but blue snagged on the peaks, a hefty grizzly was glissading on its rear end down a leftover snow bank. It had two small grizzlies on its lap. When the ride was finished, the mother and cubs rambled back up the slope. Then they slid down together again the same way. And then they did it again.

Proving that the cubs clambered onto her lap with the express intention of riding a mom toboggan would be hard. They piled on whenever she sat down or rolled onto her back, perhaps partly because a mother bear assumes those positions when nursing and partly because the little bears were constantly trying to wrestle with her. Sooner or later, all three would begin to slide downhill in one grizzled heap. In between, they chased one another, the mother galumphing this way and that in a bouncy, loose-limbed gait—floppy mode, as I call it—which turned out to be symptomatic of play, much as it is in dogs.

Until that afternoon, the grizzly lore packed into my skull since childhood was still on the rampage. I couldn't see much beyond stored-up images of bloody confrontation. It was a ferocious spell.

Watching the trio broke it. The aura of us-versus-them dissipated, as it was bound to in the presence of qualities undeniably shared. It helped that I had developed a passion for glissading down leftover snow myself. A high-speed schuss on boot soles was the payoff for many a long, hot ascent in search of goats. As often as not, I'd climb back up the snowfield to make more runs with jazzier turns. When you go to town only every few months, you have to come up with your own definition of blockbuster entertainment, like trying to coax a record number of skips from a stone flung across the reflections in an alpine lake.

The following spring, I practically glissaded into the butt of a mother grizzly that materialized on the snowfield in front of me. She had been resting in a crevice melted out next to a heat-absorbing boulder. I veered and shot past her. The bear gave chase, but the snowbank was long and steep, and she couldn't match my speed because she kept sliding around rump first. Soon, mother bear was getting too far from her new cubs, and I was no longer a threat to them, so she quit. Suppose one or two split seconds had ticked by differently. Would I have been partially disassembled? Left with seriously altered prospects for a career? With grizzlies, the answer is always Maybe. Despite that near disaster and two separate bluff charges by silvertips in the Swan Range, I never lost the feeling gained when I first met the family riding downhill together, devising their own fun high on the rim of a world that looked freshly made for as far as sight could reach.

My interest in the great bears only expanded as the years went by. And the more time I spent observing the animals, the more I found myself wondering whether people—whatever their stated intentions—would ever really allow beasts of such dimensions to be restored, and if so, how? I wound up making a sort of subcareer out of looking for answers. I imposed upon resource managers in their offices and researchers deep in the field, sought out the salmon streams and other settings where bears were said to have grown fairly used to observers, and got to know a couple of bear movie stars and asked their trainers for insight. I even went to circuses and watched bicycling bears. For the most part, I just kept roaming where grizzlies do.

Toward the end of the 1990s, I was still out traversing wildlands from southern Yellowstone to the edge of the Arctic, when I found what I realized was some of the most inventive, revealing work being done on these animals anywhere. It was a high-stakes wager on the true nature of grizz, crucial to the species' recovery, and it was taking place at home in northwestern Montana, more or less in my backyard.

TEACHING GRIZZLIES
A THING OR TWO

TIM MANLEY works for Montana's Department of Fish, Wildlife & Parks in the northwestern part of the state. He spends most of his time in the Flathead watershed, which starts practically in free fall off the Continental Divide. One of his main responsibilities is educating wild grizzly bears. This can be a chore. Tagging along as a reporter for the first time in early October of 1998, I asked Manley when he last had a day off, and he sat there pondering away in his pickup truck, stumped. He couldn't remember his last night off, either. Finally, he just put the rig in gear and drove on to find the next bear in need of instruction.

Seated by the opposite window, his equally sleep-deprived colleague, Carrie Hunt, said, "Not long ago, our man Tim here is lying in the bedroom of this woman we'd just met an hour before. He's on the floor. In the dark. With a gun. I'm loading up bullets and taking off the window screen so we'll have a clear line of fire toward her bird feeder. The whole time, I keep wondering what this scene would look like to someone who happened to walk in."

Hunt, who runs what she calls the Wind River Bear Institute, often contracts with natural resource agencies to tutor local grizz. She and Manley had a particularly intensive program under way in the Flathead region. As soon as the grizzly touched the bird feeder, they shot the creature—nailed it but good. If you're saying to yourself,

"That's about how I figured they educate bears in Montana," it's because I didn't point out that the bullets were rubber. Manley and Hunt sometimes add "cracker" shells, projectiles that detonate in the air near the target.

Frequently, in a turnabout of the usual bear tale, these humans will charge a grizzly—or grizzlies, as the case may be. One or two other people from a small, revolving cadre of paid assistants, volunteers, and visiting wildlife experts might be on hand to help out. Hunt's specially trained Karelian dogs always are. The breed, an offshoot of the Husky-Spitz line, was developed in Finland and Russia specifically to hunt bears and other big game. Invited as an observer but quickly pressed into service as a dog handler, I discovered all at once that the human part of the team makes its charge full tilt and straight on, hooting, rifles blazing, while the boldly patterned, black-and-white Karelians fan ahead on leashes attached to the handlers' waists, barking, snarling, and pulling so hard they propel the whole show even faster in multilegged spurts. It is as if the bear had stirred up a commando nest of giant, lunatic spiders.

The message is: "Who is the boldest, scariest creature with a claim to this yard? Not you. Who is dominant in such a place? Not you. Try a stunt like trespassing here, and your life fills with pain and confusion." No grizz has yet failed to heed it, and if the animal doesn't flee as quickly or far as desired, the best dogs in the bunch may be turned loose to harry its heels.

By contrast, the woman in the bedroom had been giving bears the go-ahead to act cheeky, telling them, in effect, "Here's a reward of corn, oil-rich sunflower seeds, and nice blubbery suet for coming on my lawn. Human structures and activities mean easy food. Get it?" Of course, she wasn't aware that she was communicating anything of the sort. She merely wanted to watch birds and had been regularly putting out treats for them around her house near the town of Ferndale, where the lower Swan River Valley broadens to merge with the greater Flathead Valley. She probably thought of herself as a wildlife benefactress.

Along with their polar bear cousins, grizzlies are by far the biggest, strongest predators in the New World. They can accelerate from zero to thirty or more miles per hour faster than a sports car, knock over an elk with a left hook, or drag a 1,000-pound steer off into the woods to eat like so much take-out food. What, then, are they doing hanging around bird feeders and competing with finches?

The answer begins with the fact that, while their origins and anatomy place them firmly within the carnivore order, grizzlies are consummate omnivores. With a remarkable knack for finagling hitched to their pile-driver strength, they come primed to take advantage of the most nourishing food available at any given time, be it moose, musk ox, marmot, lily bulb, crab, clam, snail, fish, mushroom, mountaintop moth aggregation, underground hornet nest, rotten carcass, fragrant herb, or freshly sprouted grass, which they will graze the livelong day in spring with all the spine-tingling drama of cows. Grizzlies own one of the longest intestinal tracts of any carnivore to help process plant roughage, and quite a few of these bears are chiefly vegetarian. As far as I know, the only large mammal able to pick from a broader menu is *Homo sapiens*. Some people eat grizz, for that matter. But then, the bears sometimes eat people, more or less evening things out.

With the onset of autumn, grizzlies enter a state known as hyperphagia. It means feeding in overdrive. They need to consume 20,000 to 30,000 calories and put on two to three pounds daily for at least a couple of months. Otherwise, they might not have sufficient energy reserves to see them through a denning period that, like the snowpack, can last half the year.

In this part of the Rockies, the ticket to Fat City is ripe huckleberries, or rather, their easily metabolized fruit sugars. But the wild crop failed badly across the mountainsides in 1998. Such a variety of weather hits the mountain West that every year seems somehow unusual. Still, people considered this one bizarre. Scores of bears headed toward lower elevations in search of alternatives such as serviceberries, chokecherries, and hawthorn fruits, all of which proved scarce as well. That left starchy roots and whatever else the bears could turn up. Eventually, the downslope search brought them to where the shrub fields and woodlands began to be replaced by rural lots.

Flathead County is roughly the size of Connecticut. A large portion consists of untenanted federal and state acreage. Nearly the entire human populace of the county resides in Flathead Valley, with about half concentrated in three small cities along the Flathead River and its tributaries. The total population comes to only around 75,000. However, this represents a 25 percent increase since 1990, and much of the growth has taken place along that interface of rural homesteads and semiwild forests.

From a historical perspective, there is nothing the least bit strange about grizzlies meandering all over the foothills and floors of Montana valleys. The most benign climates, lushest assortments of plants, and richest concentrations of animal life in the Rocky Mountains have always been found along the bottomlands. They were the heart of the great bears' original range here. But of course, that was before European Americans moved in and set about killing or displacing grizz so thoroughly that we soon began to think of them as mammals tied mainly to mountain terrain.

Nowadays, apple and plum trees weighed down by their own succulently packaged embryos awaited bears venturing lower. Livestock was trotting all over the place. The tame fruits and animals were probably unfamiliar to many grizzlies but smelled savory. And, although people were slower to grasp this, so did the sacks of feed for those horses, goats, llamas, pigs, and chickens. Even commercial rabbit chow was intriguing, as were dog food nuggets, kitty kibbles, and pellets for trout ponds. Wild scents wafted from the yards and garages of successful hunters and anglers. Ordinary household garbage amounted to grab bags of aromatic possibilities.

Where not a single one of these temptations appeared, birdseed did, all too often, leading all the way from the forest's edge to the heart of the Flathead Valley's outlying towns. Practically every second household had a feeder or two. More grain, spread for the local wild turkeys, covered the ground in places. Such troves didn't look all that different from the pine seed caches of jays and squirrels that grizzlies routinely raid in fall. Other than the education program, the only barriers between a hungry bear and a meal were the animal's normal awareness of boundaries and its inhibitions about probing too close to humans. The longer autumn wore on, the less those mattered. As far as the bear team was concerned, the grizzlies were on their way to completely devouring such things as spare time and any semblance of a personal life.

"At one point," Hunt told me, "we had ninety-two calls in two days about problem black bears and grizzlies. I'd say three-quarters of them were getting into bird feeders."

Now it was up to Hunt, a compact, loquacious, half-Argentine in her forties, and Manley, a slender Montana native whose unflappable style counterbalances Hunt's arm-waving enthusiasm, to explain all this to the woman in the bedroom. They had to help her see that she had become, like them, a teacher of grizzly bears. Next, they had to politely inform her that the course in bad habits she unwittingly offered was placing people at risk for miles around, seriously raising the odds that more bears would wind up dead at the hands of poachers, alarmed landowners, or game officials and thereby jeopardizing the recovery of an imperiled species.

Ultimately, Manley and Hunt had to convince her to do what they were asking of the grizzlies: Wise up. Pay more attention to where you live and with whom. Be a better neighbor. As you might suspect, chasing off great, fanged beasts in the dead of night can be the easy part of the job.

"She was fine, though," Manley told me. "She'd had black bears come in to the bird feeder before, and they hadn't made her nervous. This was her first grizzly. She called me the next day to see how the bear was doing."

He told her that the animal was all right and keeping out of trouble for the moment. The team was trying to guide it back toward the mountains, but it was hard to be sure where their quarry would pop up next. Manley added that they would let her know if any predicaments arose nearby and would surely appreciate it if she'd do the same for them. It would have been equally fair just to say: Lady, how do you think the bear is doing? It's a vagabond grizzly in the midst of thousands of people, and you'd better be prepared to hear that it ran into one with an itchy trigger finger. This animal is living on borrowed time.

— — —

The grizzly is the North American version of the brown bear, *Ursus arctos,* the long-clawed, hump-shouldered species also found across Eurasia from the French Pyrenees to the Japanese island of Hokkaido. Some of the trained "grizzlies" that chase after pioneer kids in movies or buddy up with mountain men on television shows are actually Syrian brown bears, which also tend to have markedly silvertipped—grizzled—fur. During mountain man times, as many as 100,000 grizzlies may have roamed the contiguous states west of the Mississippi River. In 1975, the animals were listed as threatened south of Canada because 99 percent had been eliminated there. Standing shoulder to shoulder, the remainder would scarcely have filled a used car lot.

Keystone predators, scavengers, earthmovers (those four-inch claws are mainly for digging roots and rodents), recyclers of nutrients, and distributors of seeds (from as many as 70,000 berries a day in good times), grizzlies play an outsize role in the natural communities of which they remain part. They command a similarly exaggerated niche in the human imagination. A majority of the public wants these ecological heavyweights and spawners of sagas, these mega-mammals, hauled back from the brink. The Endangered Species Act compels federal authorities to try to make that happen. Under the direction of the U.S. Fish & Wildlife Service, they have been at it for more than a quarter century now, starting with around 750 to 1,000 surviving grizzlies in the Lower 48. The current estimate is

1,000 or 1,300—marginally improved yet far from secure—and those figures are shaky.

A great deal hinges on the grizzly numbers game. Restrictions on road building and other disturbances in habitats deemed critical to the recovery of these creatures have been among the strongest, most reliable safeguards of wildlands available for many years now. In fact, the great bears have probably done more to change traditional patterns of natural resource development across much of the mountain West than any other factor except the global economy.

All kinds of industry representatives and politicians want *horribilis* declared sufficiently abundant to be taken off the imperiled list so that loggers, miners, oil wildcatters, grazers, motorized recreationists, and so on will have more leeway in national forests and other public domain. State officials generally favor optimistic counts too, since they promise a shorter wait until the feds relinquish control over the bears and Montana, Idaho, and Wyoming can manage them as big game animals again. By contrast, environmentalists are in no rush to see the grizzlies lose their shield of federal protection, especially since many in the conservation community feel that the key problem of shrinking wildland range has grown worse, not better. They are therefore inclined to view cheery projections of the bears' numbers with skepticism while embracing the more conservative estimates.

The truth is that no one knows how many grizzlies are scattered through the rugged boondocks they call home on this side of the Canadian line, and it is extremely difficult and expensive to try to find out. Population totals are fashioned from collected hair samples, which provide DNA, plus smaller numbers of actual sightings subjected to large amounts of statistical massage.

Grizzlies may live thirty years or more, crisscrossing home ranges that typically encompass several hundred square miles and occasionally more than a thousand. Even the relative homebodies among them make lengthy forays as subadults dispersing from their mothers' domains. They also make strong shifts in altitude from one season to the next, rambling between thickly forested valley floors and sun-swept tundra meadows just off the peaks. And they may move to entirely new tracts as drought, wildfires, cyclical irruptions of insects, plant disease epidemics, and normal forest succession alter the habitat mix.

It has been a long time since Americans were able to homestead in vast, untamed tracts of land out West. Grizzlies no longer have that luxury either. Most parks and designated wildernesses are too small to hold many such giants. Other preserves are too top-heavy; that is, they protect grand expanses of alpine scenery but end down where more fertile habitats start. Meanwhile—endangered species regulations notwithstanding—industry, real estate development, and mass recreation continue to extend their reach into previously remote countrysides.

What this means is that the bears have little choice but to share landscapes with us to some extent even in the best of wild-food years. Competition is inevitable and conflicts unavoidable. The question is whether they can be kept to tolerable levels. Everyone always says that the long-term solution to complex issues lies in better education. Hunt and Manley were just taking the philosophy a step farther, tutoring animals that, like us, possess a lively intelligence and inquisitive nature along with the potential for monstrous behavior.

— — —

In 1997, Hunt, Manley, and their associates worked the Karelians 160 times on thirty-one different black bears and nineteen grizzlies spread across the Montana region that grizzly biologists call the NCDE, or Northern Continental Divide Ecosystem, comprised of Glacier National Park, the Great Bear/Bob Marshall/Scapegoat Wilderness complex, and adjoining national forests, state forests, and Native American tribal lands. This year, 1998, was shaping up as the busiest yet. By early October, Manley and other wildlife officials had already been forced to capture sixteen grizzlies for vandalism, food theft, or both, in human territory. Most were released. But two, a subadult male and an adult male, were declared high-risk repeat offenders and euthanized. And eleven more grizz from the NCDE had been lost to human causes ranging from poaching to collisions with cars. Five were females, considered the population's most precious members as the bearers and nurturers of future generations.

The grizzly that Hunt and Manley spanked with rubber bullets from the woman's bedroom window was a breeding female. For proof, she had two cubs of the year at her side. Still nursing and wholly dependent upon their mother for guidance and protection, the little bears would share her fate, whatever that turned out to be. Since she seemed determined to hang around the town of Ferndale, some of the team had begun calling her Fernie.

Ferndale proper is tiny, a don't-blink-or-you'll-miss-it spot on a Montana byway. Yet it has become surrounded by a substantial collection of rural houses, trailers, and ranchettes mixed with some of the New West mansions that folks who don't have one call trophy homes or starter castles. Realtors work hard and proliferate, but the setting pretty much sells itself. Rolling hills and woods converge upon the Swan River as it winds the final miles westward toward Flathead Lake, the largest natural body of freshwater in the U.S. West. Mountain goats and alpenglow share the crest of the Swan Range along the eastern horizon. A prelude to the Great Divide, which rises on the next wave of stone to the east, the Swans mark the beginning of the wild country at the core of the NCDE.

When residents first reported Fernie to Fish, Wildlife & Parks earlier in the fall, she was raiding apples close to the Swan foothills. She had also been seen nosing around beehives. Manley strung electric fencing to guard the hives. Fernie and the cubs moved closer to the bottomlands and a subdivision at a bend in the river called Swan Horseshoe. He followed and baited a trap made from a section of steel culvert pipe. Before long, Fernie and the cubs were scratching and bawling inside it.

As it turned out, that wasn't her first experience in temporary captivity. About five years earlier, near the South Fork of the Flathead, in a bloc of national forest lands on the east side of the Swans, she had been going along just being a silvery bear in the woods, not bothering a soul, when she suddenly found herself in a trap. It had been set by Fish, Wildlife & Parks biologists as part of a general study of grizzlies under way at the time. After clamping a radio collar around her neck, the researchers duly labeled her Grizzly Bear No. 21 and released her to serve as a beacon of data.

The batteries that power such transmitters last no longer than a couple of years, and the collars are designed to drop off afterward to spare the bears a lifelong encumbrance. By the time Bear No. 21 made her way over the crest of the Swans and down toward Ferndale, she was long gone from the airwaves. Her fur bore no trace of having worn a radio necklace. Only after Manley nabbed her and noticed an old tag affixed to one ear did her past come to light. He gave her another collar so he could keep close tabs on her movements, a standard policy with grizz that become problematic. He then transported the trio back to the South Fork and released them in the Battery Creek drainage, part of Fernie's—Bear No. 21's—original range.

The female and her cubs promptly took off for points east. That meant negotiating Hungry Horse Reservoir, formed where the South Fork of the Flathead River backs up behind Hungry Horse Dam. The artificial lake is between one and two miles wide. Although grizzlies are reasonably good swimmers, Manley was somewhat surprised to record cubs of the year paddling across, especially Fernie's cubs. Possibly reflecting the poor nourishment available to their nursing mother, the youngsters couldn't have weighed much over forty-five pounds, whereas typical first-year grizz are in the seventy-five- to one-hundred-pound range by autumn. Shortly afterward, Fernie's radio signal indicated that the three had turned around and swum back across the reservoir to the west side. Then, to Manley's astonishment, they swam it a third time, revisiting the east shore.

"My guess is that they couldn't find anything to eat," he recalled. "They were searching all over the place, swimming laps across the reservoir and running themselves ragged. There's just no food in the usual places this year. They kept on moving and showed up toward the head of the reservoir, scrounging around the Spotted Bear Ranger Station. We got the call and cracker-shelled them out of there." Within twenty-four hours, the bears had beelined the fifteen miles or so back to Battery Creek. From there, Fernie once more led her offspring westward over the Swan divide to the Swan Valley and on into trouble.

Hunt said, "The cubs came back noticeably smaller than they were before they got moved to the South Fork. They've been out there losing weight when they're supposed to be fattening up for winter. One cub looks seriously undersize to me. If we trap and relocate them again, they'll just come back, and all we'll have done is add stress and knock down their energy reserves still further. Mom is saying, 'Hey, I need to be here. I can find food here. I tried my best out there, and I couldn't do it. If I'm going to keep producing milk and feed these babies, I've got to take my chances down in the valley right now.'"

"We aren't really sure what the rules ought to be in a year like this," Manley said, referring to the severe shortage of natural foods. "Nobody is. We're in new management territory here."

State and federal wildlife agencies had made real strides toward eliminating the worst of the unnatural attractants in occupied grizzly habitat. They had transferred sheep grazing allotments out of remote public lands, helped find alternatives to the livestock graveyards called bone piles, where ranchers deposit carcasses from their herds, and encouraged municipalities to enclose open landfills. The old trash Dumpsters and garbage cans in townsites next to parks and other bear strongholds were being replaced by bear-proof versions. Guidelines for keeping a clean camp reached backpackers, car-borne tourists, hunters, guides, and outfitters alike through signs and brochures. Local papers and television stations passed along similar tips to the region's populace in general, using the slogan "A Fed Bear Is a Dead Bear" as a reminder.

Some citizens actually paid attention. The remainder continued going about their lives in customary fashion, which is to say, as if they themselves were the only large omnivores worth thinking about. Put another way, they inspired almost every bear management expert I ever met to tell me that the main challenge is not managing bears, it's managing people.

A female grizzly doesn't give birth for the first time until age four or five and usually produces cubs only every third year thereafter. This gives the species one of the lowest rates of reproduction among mammals and represents a bottleneck for recovery efforts. Accordingly, wildlife managers have been inclined to give troublemaking mother grizz a break. Where a single serious offense such as damaging buildings sometimes has condemned a male to lethal injection or internment at a zoo, females have generally been granted at least two chances to screw up.

The conventional response to even minor infractions of rules—remaining conspicuous near human settlement, for instance—has been to catch the offending bear and haul it off to be released in a different, less crowded stretch of country, as was done to Fernie and her cubs. This strategy of exile has always had two fundamental flaws. The first and foremost is that unless a grizzly is set loose more than a couple hundred miles distant, it can find its way back, often within a week or two. A few transplants, especially younger bears that hadn't yet carved out a home range, might stick around the new site. But if resident grizzlies don't soon drive the newcomers out, hunger plus unfamiliarity with the terrain and the whereabouts of natural foods usually will. Twice displaced now, they are likely to wind up scavenging human supplies again, just doing it in someone else's bailiwick. That is the second flaw.

"For God's sake, why don't we use a little common sense and put those problem grizzlies so far back in the wilderness that they can't bother anybody?" The suggestion, which managers hear constantly, sounds logical. But it is a form of denial. Reared on the frontier myth, Americans can't quite seem to come to terms with the fact that there is no such place left in the Lower 48. To trek out to the nearest road or pasture from the most remote spot in any park or wilderness would take a human in good physical shape only two or three days. For a bear, it's more like a jaunt.

Transplanting grizzlies with a rap sheet has been a low percentage deal all around. Whether the policy was one, two, or three strikes and you're out, control actions were still leading, in the end, to a death sentence or life behind bars. And with human population growth in scenic portions of the rural West surging twice as fast as the national average, more silvertips kept falling because of poachers, mistaken black-bear hunters, deer and elk hunters suddenly confronted over meat they had downed, panicked landowners claiming defense of life and property, collisions with trains and automobiles barreling through key habitat corridors, and a welter of other miscues resulting from the intersection of bears' lives and ours. As a result, annual losses in the wild populations too often exceeded the guidelines for recovery, particularly those set for breeding females.

Bear managers sorely needed some way out of the spiral. That was why, when Carrie Hunt proposed working with grizzlies' learning abilities to correct problem behavior, she wasn't laughed clean out of cowboy country. As goofy as educating grizz sounded to some of the hardcore hook-and-bullet boys in game departments and to other members of the old guard, a few officials were willing to take a chance. They preferred to speak of it as adding one more tool to the kit.

Fish, Wildlife & Parks may have signed on to this business of trying to school bears, but Fernie was enough to give the most enlightened department head fits. She was raiding too many places and testing too many homeowners' nerves. Even with the extra latitude granted female grizz on probation under the bear team's watch, the protocol jointly developed by state and federal bear experts now demanded that she be removed from the population to ensure the safety and welfare of the public.

Manley went to his bosses in the state wildlife agency to plead for a reprieve. His argument ran as follows: We've been locked into our two standards for male and female bears deemed troublemakers. Yet we understand grizzlies a lot better than we used to, and one of the main things we've learned is how different each individual can be from the next. As far as money and manpower allow, we need to try making these life-or-death calls case by case, grizz by grizz. It would give all of us some more breathing room.

Yes, Fernie's all over the rural suburbs, Manley said, but this is not a dangerous bear. She's a nice bear—a gentle bear. All you have to do is shout at Fernie, and she lopes away into cover. She hasn't shown the least sign of aggression toward people. Not once. Even for a female interior grizzly, she's slightly on the small side. At 250 to 260 pounds, the animal is lighter than the average front lineman on a pro football team.

So we're not exactly talking about some True Testosterone Tales version of the species. (There I was, staring up into the blood-drenched jaws of a veritable mountain of grizzly fury!) And we have the overriding circumstance to consider: who can remember a year when berries and pine nuts and other natural foods were this sparse? Cut her a bit more slack, Manley implored. If we can get her through two or three more weeks until den-up time, we'll be one breeding female closer to meeting our recovery goal.

That all sounds reasonable, agreed the decision makers, even compelling. But what if you're wrong? Or suppose you're basically right but something goes haywire, as it could in a split second, and she ends up hurting or killing someone? Even if she never ruffles one hair on one person's head, having a mother grizzly continue to run around between houses tearing up things to get at food is lousy public relations. The agencies look inept at handling problems, and Fernie's raids aren't doing the grizzly's image much good either. Rather than advance recovery, she could set back support for the effort. So tell us again why we have to give this animal a reprieve.

Because we're dealing with a bad year, not a bad bear, Manley insisted. We'll have someone on Fernie all the time, following the radio signal. We're ready to step in with the guns and dogs and tell her where she's allowed to be and where she isn't. We're contacting every resident we can so they're on board. This is a test I think we can pass. Give us at least some more days to see how things go, and I'll keep you posted up to the minute.

Okay, we'll play it by guess and by God, said the agency higher-ups, disproving the claim that all bureaucrats are ruled by the reflex to duck and cover. Everybody's rear end was going to be hanging over the edge right along with Fernie's. They didn't know it yet, but Manley would be back, asking them to lean out farther.

MIDNIGHT WITH
BEAR-BEAR AND STAHR

To GET UP TO speed on the grizzly education project, I was constantly scribbling down background information from the teachers as we bounced along back roads in their pickup truck. I could hardly read my own writing, but it helped pass the miles. We had started a new day homing in on the radio frequencies of Fernie and other bears footloose between Ferndale and the nearby village of Bigfork, where the Swan River empties into Flathead Lake. In the absence of any immediate crises, an assistant crew came in to take over the monitoring work. Tim Manley, Carrie Hunt, and I were now about seventy miles north of them, fifteen miles south of Canada, and one mile west of Glacier National Park, following the dusty, washboard-ribbed, potholed road that runs along the North Fork of the Flathead River.

Manley had the wheel. Hunt periodically tuned to different frequencies on the receiver, trying to pick up signals from any of the several grizz that had been causing headaches in this part of the region. Behind us, in the camper on the truck bed, half a dozen restless Karelians made their presence known by thumps and the scritching of claws on linoleum.

The North Fork is a National Wild & Scenic River, and the valley that holds it is long, heavily forested, and remote. Just across the border in southeasternmost British Columbia, Canada, the upper North Fork appears to hold the thickest concentration of grizzlies yet recorded in Canada's interior. The U.S. side may harbor more grizz per square mile than anyplace else in the Lower 48.

Population density figures for this species vary dramatically from one range to the next. To me, this reinforces the notion that there is no such thing as a standard grizzly, for whenever you generalize about the animals' favorite kind of country or how often they encounter each other, you are bound to be way off for many a bear. Some tundra stretches of Alaska's North Slope and the Canadian Arctic support just one grizzly for every several hundred square miles. Yet along coastal terrain veined with streams that host a succession of salmon runs through summer and fall, biologists have recorded an average of between one and two grizzlies for each square mile. This is why even though it is still true that the great majority of occupied grizzly range lies in the continent's interior, at least half the grizzlies alive today are within about 100 miles of the Pacific. Hotspots such as Kodiak Island, the Alaska Peninsula, and Admiralty Island in the southeastern part of the forty-ninth state are the big-bear equivalents of New Delhi or teeming Hong Kong.

Asked to name America's premier grizz country outside of Alaska, many Americans would say Yellowstone. The area has about one silvertip for every twenty to forty square miles. Key sections of the North Fork host one for every five to ten square miles. The valley also supports a robust cougar population, and it was here that natural recolonization of the western United States by wolves got under way, beginning in the late 1970s and early 1980s. They share the terrain with lynx, bobcat, marten, fisher, wolverine, river otter, badger, mink, various weasels, coyote, red fox, and black bear. As ecologist John Weaver pointed out in a recent report, *The Transboundary Flathead*, what emerges is a carnivore community "unmatched in North America for its variety, completeness, use of valley bottomlands, and density of species which are rare elsewhere."

In the U.S. portion of this valley, everything east of the river lies within Glacier National Park. Nearly all the western side is state or national forest land that eventually rises to the crest of the Whitefish

Range. The remaining fraction consists of privately owned parcels. Scattered along the valley floor and atop benchlands immediately to the west, they are occupied by a couple hundred people in the warmer months but by fewer than fifty year-round. One of the valley floor properties belongs to me and Karen Reeves, my wife.

~ ~ ~

After I quit studying mountain goats, I still wanted to live close to the peaks and someplace with more big wild animals than people nearby. Karen and I chose the North Fork. During the mid-1970s, we built a log cabin on acreage immediately across the river from the park. It was our full-time home for about eleven years, and we reared two children there. Once they reached school age, we moved to the town of Whitefish in the Flathead Valley to put them in classes, but we still have the land and stay there when we can. A Wild & Scenic River conservation easement arranged through the U.S. Forest Service guarantees that the habitat will always remain more or less as it is.

Soon after settling along the North Fork, Karen and I developed a pattern of hiking through a series of natural clearings over on the valley's park side. We did this on and off throughout the year. During the incomparably new mornings of spring, at least one of us was usually out before dawn.

Game paths led through lodgepole pines and their brown, winter-matted understory and then spread out through openings awash in early growth. Set against glittering backdrops of mountainsides still buried beneath snow, the meadows seemed all the more tenderly green. The animal community drawn to these oases so often included grizzly bears that our glands would have us pumped full of thrill juices before we were partway there. Walking in half-light, we moved very slowly, pausing to listen every few steps. If all we found at the end were mountain bluebirds and ground squirrels, it was still a splendid way to get a jump on the day and put its other challenges in perspective.

I saw grizzlies courting in a meadow one morning in May. Karen went alone the next day and watched a pair indulge in the same sort of chasing and carefully modulated roughhousing. They went on to mate. Afterward, she told me, they grazed the green-up side by side, bumping shoulders, and strolled the perimeter, nuzzling a bit.

A week later, I found a grizzly by itself in the same meadow. The ends of its hairs had the characteristic frosting of silver, but the roots were quite dark, almost black when in shade. It was a big animal with an elongated frame and a slightly longer-than-usual muzzle. These are all features I tend to associate with males—without a lot of justification. Unless you happen to see the angle at which a grizzly urinates or notice a tuft of long hairs in the vaginal area (I hope you're doing this through a telescope), it is extremely difficult to tell the sex of a solitary animal in the field. Nevertheless, the largest males do grow larger than the largest females by at least a couple hundred pounds, and this grizzly looked immense for the Rockies.

I was in a good position more than 100 yards away, crouched behind young trees on the cuff of the forest and slightly uphill. The bear had no chance to see me, and the air was perfectly still. As the morning brightened, the growing warmth brought out fragrances of frost-worked earth, conifer needles, crushed sprouts, and fresh pellet piles of elk dung. Raven calls arose from deep in the trees. Intent upon eating sedge shoots and the basal portions of young cow parsnip in a meltwater-soaked depression, the grizzly moved very little. Willow branches grew out of that wet ground, and I could see the first yellow warblers to arrive back in the country flashing among them like harbingers of the sun.

By crawling a few feet to either side of my post, I kept an eye on the rest of the meadow to find out what else the bear and I had for company. Ground squirrels not long out of winter dormancy popped up from burrows—and dove back down with piercing whistles, for a pair of coyotes patrolled the middle of the main colony, swiveling their heads as if overwhelmed by possibilities.

Small groups of white-tailed deer grazed near the opposite side of the opening. They seemed unconcerned about the coyotes, but their ears were in constant motion. Every few seconds, one's head would jerk upright, sometimes followed by the tail—the warning flag—and several deer would float along in a high-stepping trot before settling down again. Just before the first sunlight slanted through the conifers onto the arena, a band of elk passed through, casting glances from side to side. A smaller grizzly briefly emerged from the willow brush that outlined another boggy streak. This bear kept nervously peering around and testing the air the entire time it was visible.

And all the while, the dark grizzly kept its nose down in the green. If the big bear looked up more than twice in an hour, I missed it. By comparison with all the skittering and scanning going on around it, the animal seemed downright phlegmatic. At last, it raised its head and took a lengthy look and sniff. But its feet barely shifted, and it resumed feeding without glancing up for another half hour.

For most of that interlude, I thought it was the dullest grizzly I had ever watched. I felt the first hint of wind and prepared to leave before I could be detected. Only after I had taken a few steps toward home did I understand what I had beheld. The bear wasn't lethargic. It simply had no reason to act concerned. About anything. Within the park, it was insulated from harm at the hands of people. No humans were nearby anyway, other than myself. Nor were any larger, higher-ranking bears around—if such bears existed. I was looking at an animal that could kick anybody's and everybody's ass from here to the summits and back if it came to that.

I had heard the expression "master of all he surveys" most of my life. Now I had met him—or, just maybe, her. In keeping with the fine irony that seems to reside at the heart of things, the master, the monarch, of all he surveyed didn't need to survey much at all. He ate. He thought his bear thoughts. He surveyed at his pleasure.

When we hear the word *grizzly*, each of us conjures up a different image of a bear for a host of private reasons. The bear in the meadow is often the one that comes to mind for me. It is how I like to think of a grizzly and its life. I know that the individual I watched was, in many ways, an exception. But—as I came to appreciate more with each hike—every grizzly is.

— — —

During those early years of our North Fork cabin life, the great bears had recently been declared threatened, and their numbers and habitat were still slipping. It seemed at times that my generation might be the last one south of Canada able to watch and marvel at these animals' lives—the last for whom grizzlies, with all the sensations of heightened alertness, power, beauty, fear, and delight they call into being, would be part of the meaning of being outdoors. Would ours be the final cycle of grizz stories, then?

Now, while I sat squeezed between the bear educators, the truck ground uphill onto a North Fork benchland not far from my cabin, and the rattles and squeaks in a cab full of loose rifle cartridge boxes, clipboards with data sheets, rolling thermoses, pens, and flashlights were suddenly overridden by an insistent radio signal. It came from a young female grizzly named Daryl. She had lately taken to feeding in an area burned by a 1988 forest fire. The regenerating ground cover included pealike vetch with starchy roots and some kinnikinnick, or bearberry, which puts out small, mealy fruits. These plants grew there because the site was fairly open. Unfortunately for Daryl, it was also close to the road in places, exposing her to occasional traffic.

"If we hear of a grizzly hanging around too close to a road or trail but still behaving naturally, we have no reason to jump all over that animal," Hunt said. "We want to let it know, 'What you're doing is okay; you just need to do it farther away.' We'll clap and yell and maybe bark the bear [have the dogs shout at it] a little. If it stays where it is or comes closer, we pump up the volume. But as soon as it moves the other direction, we stop. The idea is to make it easy for a bear to do the right thing and hard for it to do the wrong thing.

"Daryl is an example of a grizzly we didn't find out about quite soon enough," Hunt concluded with a shrug, meaning that the grizzly had already become habituated to the sight and sound of passing automobiles. From that stage, it was a short leap to foraging comfortably around other kinds of human goings-on.

With most of the big trees fallen and the rest charred bare, the fire-cleared benchland offered a spectacular georama of the Livingstone Range in Glacier. Several people had built new cabins there to take advantage of the view. Blade, Daryl's brother, often used the same area. The education team put both siblings in school and did not spare the discipline. They seemed to be responding, keeping farther from the road and away from homes. But while Blade moved off to less disturbed portions of the range, Daryl had not. She was merely getting better at staying out of sight. That wasn't great, Hunt declared, but it was acceptable.

The use of disturbing, frightening, or downright painful stimuli to teach an animal to avoid specific objects or places is known as *aversive conditioning*. Another term is *negative reinforcement*. Hunt relies heavily on this process to modify behavior, but she prefers to call what she does "bear shepherding" to downplay the punitive aspect. To be fair, a good deal of the work is simply a matter of following a grizzly to find out what it's doing, then rushing to catch up and shepherd the creature one direction or another at critical junctures.

"The dogs give us the option of going right at a bear in the open," said Hunt. "There's no way we would try that on certain grizzlies or in certain situations without dogs. The risk of inciting a charge is too high. That could leave us with nothing but a dead bear, not to mention the possibility of getting somebody torn up."

Never one to neglect the public awareness and fund-raising aspects of the task at hand, Hunt named her program Partners in Life. Those words run across the bottom of a logo displayed on the team's baseball caps, vehicles, and handout literature. Across the top is an exhortation: Teach Your Bears Well. In the logo's center is a portrait of a Karelian with a no-nonsense stare.

We drove back and forth as the afternoon faded, waiting to see what Daryl, a C student in need of improvement, might do next. She never showed herself, confining most of her movements to the bottom of a draw and the far end of the opening. That alone temporarily boosted her grade and allowed the bear team to break off and continue north. Within half an hour, we were parked near a male grizzly named Louie. He was in a fairly recent, boondocks-style subdivision, where someone had split a large wooded tract into parcels of a few acres each sold as cabin sites. The trees had been thinned around one unoccupied new building. Louie was grazing what was left of the clover seeded among stumps in the yard.

The coloration of his plush fall coat was classic for the region: deep brown toward the roots with yellow tones along the sides and back and an overall patina of silver. Depending upon the light's strength and the angle from which you viewed him, the grizzly was the color of wood one moment, charcoal the next, and then gold. And all the while, the lambent tips of the fur made him seem to be moving within an aura, as if he were radiating power.

A three-year-old (since biologists categorize bears as cubs, yearlings, two-year-olds, and so on, a three-year-old is actually in its fourth year of life), Louie was not an impressively large bear. He was nevertheless highly conspicuous on this acreage and so little concerned about it that a few locals had been dropping by to watch him. The team felt that Louie was starting to take humans way too lightly, however recent their claim to this spot might be. He had broken into an unoccupied cabin elsewhere, one with a blood trail leading to the door and a deer carcass strung up inside. So after a good, long bear-watching session of our own, we banged and barked him off into the woods.

We stayed on into early evening to make sure Louie kept away. Finally, at Hunt's signal, the dogs piled into the camper. Manley drove back to the main road. Within minutes, he steered onto another side route, and Hunt tuned to the frequency of Stahr, a female grizzly with one cub of the year. A couple of miles up the creek drainage, the receiver began issuing strong, regular beeps. Hunt switched from the truck's roof-mounted whip antenna, which picks up radio waves at a considerable distance but provides no clue as to their location, to a handheld antenna shaped like a T. She thrust that out the window, slowly rotating the elements back and forth to determine where the strongest signal was coming from. As the direction became clear, she turned to Manley with a resigned look on her face. Dusk had given way to night, and Stahr was right where they hoped she would not be.

Our dust plume drifted across the truck's headlights as we pulled up to a solitary cabin in a phalanx of larch and lodgepole pine. The resident, I'd been told, was another single woman. Yet two figures appeared through the luminous haze. Apparently, a woman from down the road was paying a call. I stayed behind when Manley and Hunt walked over to talk to the pair. In the dark, I remained confused about identities. Both the locals were waving lit cigarettes as they spoke, and, from the snatches of conversation I could make out, both had lately been dealing with overly inquisitive grizz.

One of the women stood in that backcountry night forest wearing a pink, ruffled housecoat and holding some kind of lapdog. I heard a voice say, "Well, I *am* starting to get kind of nervous about this bear." That was followed by a high-pitched, crooning voice distinct from all the others. Was there a person here I hadn't seen? No. I realized that the lady in pink had started talking to her little pooch. She was calling it "Bear-Bear" and "Pepe le Bear."

Bigger dogs ranged the yard, where plastic chew toys molded into the shape of hot dogs and cheese wheels were strewn about. One lanky hound had a wound on its leg from tangling with Stahr several days earlier. I switched on the radio receiver inside the truck. The pulses from Stahr's collar came booming in.

Beep. Beep. Beep. Chweep. Chweep. CHWEEP. CHWEEP! CHWEEP! CHWEEP! . . .

I detached the coaxial cable from the antenna and held the cable's plug end out into the night air. If you can still detect a signal this way, it means the source is quite close.

Chweep! Chweep! Chweep! Chweep!

Stahr might have been taking in the scene from not much farther away than I was.

When I joined the group and introduced myself, the cabin's owner—I'll call her Flo—told me of opening the door to her front porch and walking in on this grizzly. "It was laying right there on the couch," she said. "Luckily, when it ran, it ran out instead of on into the house." Stahr had been cozied up next to plundered sacks of dog food. She hit a jackpot. The porch had held 300 pounds of nuggets.

That, it turned out, was an earlier raid. Flo's most recent call was to report that Stahr had returned and tried pushing in the porch door. As the bear team reviewed the incident with her, they discovered that Flo had been away on another errand, and, although she had taken the trouble to latch the porch door this time, she had left the dog food out on the porch floor. Again.

Manley and Hunt had already come to check on this cabin fifteen different times. They sat outside in their truck five complete nights, hoping for an opportunity to chastise Stahr. Flo either couldn't remember to move the dogs' food and dishes into the main house or she couldn't be bothered. She also kept horse grain pellets in a detached barn-garage. While I watched, a quick check by Manley determined that Flo had, as ever, failed to secure the food. This woman just was not getting the picture. Stahr was. The bear had been out snacking in the garage.

CHWEEP! CHWEEP! CHWEEP! CHWEEP!

Precious little escapes a grizzly's peerless nose. Now that Stahr had inadvertently been trained to include the cabin site in her foraging circuit, she was going to remain aware of where the food was. The issue was how readily she could get at it. As a full-time professional grizzly and nursing mother, Stahr's job was to be where the most calories were easiest to come by. Whether that was here, some other cabin, or the wild was up to Flo and her neighbors.

For the umpteenth time, the bear team reviewed with Flo the commonsense procedures for keeping attractants to a minimum. If she didn't want to move the food in the barn, Manley said, he would drive up another day and string electric fencing around the building. She said not to bother. The neighbor allowed as how she had to be going. Flo went back into the house, and the team retired to the truck to begin night number six of waiting for Stahr and her cub to show themselves.

When I asked about Stahr's history, Manley warned me that it was woven from if's and maybe's. Back in 1995, he said, Fish, Wildlife & Parks personnel heard reports from the North Fork of a female grizzly with a new cub close to the road and cabins. The following year, a female and a yearling cub were reported lingering by one particular home. It sounded like the same pair. They were acting as though they had already obtained food from human territory and were likely to continue the pattern.

Manley thought he had better get a radio on this female. He brought in the most common and efficient type of trap, one made from large-diameter culvert pipe and attached to a trailer bed so it can be towed from spot to spot. When a bear enters and tugs on the bait, an attached wire trips a heavy sliding door, and the animal is shut into the man-made, mobile cave.

In less accessible areas, biologists rely on foot snares made of flexible airplane cable, which can easily be carried in. Each is anchored to a stout tree and then buried along with a spring-loaded trigger beneath a shallow covering of dirt and leaf litter. The next step involves adding some outrageous scent concoction on the order of rotted slaughterhouse blood mixed with puree of really foul fish and a soupçon of beaver gland or deer liver or something. And whether the snare setter is a man or a woman, a zoologist with advanced degrees or an undergraduate assistant, this person will become as coy as an old fur trapper about revealing the exact ingredients, even while swearing that they add up to a brew no grizz can resist. The gunk is dribbled about, sometimes with bait. Extra brew with an even more attention-getting pungency like ammonia may be strung high overhead to spread its aroma in the breeze. Below, logs, boughs, and pointed stakes are artfully arranged to guide an arriving bear's foot precisely to a hidden cable loop.

Snare traps work well, though the struggle to escape can take a lot out of a grizz. Black bears caught in them tend to give up after a while and await their fate. They back away and often cringe when people approach. In contrast, a grizzly will tear the earth until a deep crater circles the anchor tree. Every smaller tree within reach will be felled, smashed, and chewed into matchsticks. And when people draw near, the grizzly detonates all over again. I've seen a couple of them hit the end of the cable so hard that they turned double somersaults. Injuries to the ankles and feet are not common, but they occur, and a grizz held only by the toes may rip some off in its frenzy to be free.

In the case of a bear grown too savvy to enter a trap or one that has to be immediately removed from, say, the middle of town, managers will try to free-range it—shoot the animal with a drug-bearing dart. Since immobilizing chemicals can take several minutes to kick in, the trick is to catch up with a fleeing bear before it disappears somewhere to sleep off the injection. Worse, the animal could stagger off a cliff or stumble into water and drown as it loses muscle control. An adverse reaction or overdose requiring quick administration of an antidote is always a possibility as well. By the same token, a biologist could underestimate a grizzly's weight, deliver too small a dose, and race into the brush after his target only to find it in possession of all its considerable faculties. Obviously, having a few Karelians to handle the tracking and make the first contact can be a priceless advantage.

Manley had no success at capturing the mother and yearling with any method before another winter blanketed the valley, enforcing peace in the entwined affairs of humans and great bears.

Spring of 1997 brought a female grizzly down from high on the mountainsides, where these animals typically den beneath a deep, insulating cover of snow. On a partially cleared stretch of benchland overlooking the North Fork's broad valley floor lived a wildlife photographer. The man regularly strewed bushels of grain in the yard by his brand-new cabin and pond. Some of the food was for wintering deer, he maintained, and the rest for migrating waterfowl and small forest creatures, not for luring in grizzlies for pictures, though he took plenty when they came. Either way, he persisted despite being cautioned. Hunt and Manley figured that seven or eight different grizzlies got hooked on his handouts to some extent, and the female was one of them.

That fall, by a cabin several miles south, a grizzly tried breaking into a kennel that held three dogs and their food. Manley wheeled in with a culvert trap and got the bear to enter that instead. It proved to be a female. He thought he recognized her from the photographer's place, and he had a strong hunch that she was the cabin-yard loiterer he had tried unsuccessfully to catch the previous year. But because Manley couldn't be positive, the grizzly got the same treatment that many other first-time offenders do these days. He knocked her out with drugs long enough to perform routine measurements and a general check on her condition and to fasten a radio collar around her neck. Then he turned her loose where she had been captured.

On-site releases reflect both a new way of thinking about grizzlies and the generally poor success of efforts to relocate them. It's a bit like the difference between facing your problems and shoving them aside in the hope that they will somehow disappear. Unless an individual bear appears too brazen or surly to be left anywhere near the scene of its mischief, its best hope for survival is to stay where it is familiar with the terrain, the patches of seasonal foods, and the travel routes between them. To its home range knowledge, the bear needs to add new information about where it shouldn't go and what it is not supposed to do. Instilling that information is the bear team's job.

As a rule, an on-site release will be accompanied by a lot of barking and screaming, banging on the steel culvert, and maybe a final smack on the rump with a rubber bullet as the bear skedaddles away from the opened door. The point is to make the animal associate that location with a miserable hiatus in its normal existence. Being captured, frustrated, poked with hypodermics, and thoroughly manhandled is, in itself, enough of a negative experience to set some bears on the path of righteousness. The team will find out soon enough. They try to stick right behind the parolee so they can instantly do some additional aversive conditioning, which they like to call booster work, if the animal starts to relapse.

The other part of rehabilitation is minimizing temptations in the area, and that is the local residents' job. What the bear team can do as they visit homes during the course of tracking is offer suggestions and pitch in to help secure food. And keep swapping grizz stories—taking in the ones most every Montanan has, even if they are only second- or thirdhand, and handing back true ones. With luck, the team can get people interested enough in the fate of the individual animals nearby to go on making an extra effort of their own. In a way, the team members are like door-to-door missionaries, spreading the One Simple Truth, which they repeat like a chant: If you keep your place clean, 95 percent of all our bear problems will vanish like the snow in spring.

As Manley set the female free along the North Fork, the Wind River Bear Institute folks decided to name her Stahr, after the owner of the place with the kennel. Within the week, roughly eight miles north by the recent subdivision with clover in the yard, Manley captured a newly independent two-year-old male grizzly and put him on the air as well. That was the bear he named Louie.

Stahr went back to the photographer's home. The team worked her hard with the Karelians and nonlethal rifle fire, striving to sever the connection she had made between this human setting and handy meals. They learned that the man had been snapping images of the bears rummaging in his yard for more years than they previously had known about. When he showed the inwardly fuming team more of his pictures, it became apparent that not seven or eight but a dozen different grizzlies had been coming around his place.

In the eyes of the bear teachers, this guy was contributing to the delinquency of grizzlies for profit, setting them on the road to ruin in order to boost picture sales. Whether this is what he intended or not, neighbors up and down the valley, like the fellow with the kenneled dogs, had to deal with the consequences. Manley and Hunt were spending half their waking hours doing the same, and they had more waking hours than anyone ought to have. They wanted to haul the photographer into court for the legal equivalent of a good spanking with rubber bullets, as did a number of North Forkers, but they knew that the chances were virtually nil.

Montana laws in regard to feeding wildlife are few and weak.

Nobody pays much attention to them, even though recent state legislation did finally attempt to put more teeth in the rules. There are strong federal statutes that specifically prohibit harming or harassing imperiled animals, and accustoming grizzlies to human food can ultimately prove as lethal as poison. But while agency officials might take pride in spreading pamphlets with the slogan "A Fed Bear Is a Dead Bear," they weren't about to actually bust someone for leaving out corn or garbage or, for that matter, dog chow. Intent to harm would be almost impossible to prove, and the case would likely succeed only in fueling Western resentment toward government regulations and the Endangered Species Act in particular.

One worthwhile thing did come out of the long-standing food-fest around the photographer's cabin. From the man's pictures, Manley not only recognized Stahr when she was younger but realized that the offspring trailing behind her in 1995 and 1996 looked very much like Louie. Now that both were on the airwaves, he found Louie shadowing Stahr during her travels up and down the North Fork. Evidently, Louie was not quite as independent as subadults were assumed to be after leaving their mother, and it was a fresh insight into the species.

In late autumn, Stahr crossed the river into the haven of Glacier Park and climbed the flanks of the Livingstone Range toward Longbow Lake. A week later, Louie followed much the same route. Almost certain by then that Stahr was the mystery bear he had tried to catch, and that Louie was her old cub, Manley has wondered ever since if the two reunited at any point before denning in the same area.

When Stahr emerged from her den in the spring of 1998, she had three new offspring at her heels. Dropping to lower elevations, they came upon a park garbage bin made bear-proof by dint of a recessed latch system. Perhaps Stahr's experience with filching human provisions from assorted containers was what allowed her to redefine bear proof. Or maybe she was just smarter than the average bear. She opened the contraption, introduced her cubs to garbage, and then left the park for the valley's western side. Only this time, she crossed the river on a bridge; her babies were still quite small, and she was probably unwilling to subject them to the runoff waters roiling over the North Fork's banks.

Resuming life in the patchwork of national forest lands and private holdings just beyond the park boundary, Stahr soon found food in barns and around houses. The pattern continued through the summer. "At that point," Manley told me, "she was basically raising three cubs on porch food." During the early weeks of the hungry, hectic, berryless fall of 1998, Stahr was seen with only two cubs. Whether a male grizzly, cougar, wolf pack, or accident claimed the missing youngster was anybody's guess. It might have starved.

While Hunt and Manley were away at a meeting the last week of September, a different bear manager from Fish, Wildlife & Parks trapped the diminished bear family at Flo's. But the operation went badly. One cub got a paw slammed in the heavy culvert trap door. The little bear pulled loose, only to be injured again when the manager free-ranged it as it clung to a tree, and the cub fell twenty feet to the ground. A check of the drugged animal failed to turn up any obvious broken bones, so the manager proceeded to transport all three grizzlies into the park. They were let go in the Anaconda Creek drainage. Within a short time, the mother was back in her west side haunts, raiding. Only one cub still followed.

People naturally tended to view Stahr's ongoing quest for nourishment in terms of their own inconvenience and aggravation, night worries, thrills, chills, messes to clean up, and grizz tales to tell. There was no denying that Stahr was making a major nuisance of herself—being a big, dangerous pain in the neck. At the same time, it was also clear that this female and her surviving youngster were absorbed in a desperate struggle for their lives.

— — —

Stahr's signal stayed loud outside the woman's lonely cabin. But the grizzly never revealed herself. Having already picked the place, the bear had apparently learned to bide her time. I sat huddled in the pickup, staring sleepy-lidded at the house beneath silent mountains and a night sky unsullied by lights from any town, thinking that whatever else Flo was, she must be fairly gutsy. Then again, maybe she had an unreasonable faith in her dogs.

This being mid-October in Montana, the temperature plunged as the hours wore on. Midnight passed, and the thermometer sank farther below the freezing mark. The truck windows were icing over. I was about to pull my head down inside my coat and try to snooze when Manley spoke up. He said, "You think you can't do another long night or an extra trip to check up on a bear, but then you do it. You have to ask yourself what a bear's life is worth."

The minutes crept along dark and cold and silent before he added, "I don't have unrealistic expectations. I know we're not going to save every bear out there. You just do all you can."

It looked as though no matter how long we waited, though, Stahr wasn't going to come prowling. If anything, she seemed to have withdrawn a ways to the north. Manley finally started the engine, and we left the cabin site in our taillights. While the stars wheeled on between the peaks, we drove around trying to pin down the wee-hour whereabouts of Louie and Daryl. "They're being good," Hunt concluded, marking a map with current radio locations fairly well separated from human territory. The team moved on to check on a culvert trap set for a bear that had been poking around the Polebridge Mercantile Store, which served as the valley's post office and social hub, and an assortment of cabins next door.

From there, it was a short drive to the park ranger station, where we threw down our sleeping bags and collapsed. At least, I did. Tireless on the subjects of dogs, bears, strategies for shaping behaviors, and plans in general, Hunt was still holding forth about something as I knocked on the door of dreamland and begged to be let in.

Way too early, our little group was up and moving back to Flo's. The woman had told us she would be leaving for town that day. Betting that her absence would encourage Stahr to try a raid, Manley and Hunt intended to deliver a memorable lesson. I hid with Hunt in a generator shed near the house. Manley took up position near the barn. Ted Woods, a freelance photographer on assignment for *Smithsonian* magazine, sat in the pickup truck focusing a long lens on the front door of Flo's cabin. Then we started waiting again.

Chweep! Chweep! Chweep! Chweep!

Stahr's signal came in clearly yet softly, for Hunt had turned the volume on her portable receiver down fairly low. I pressed close to the shed's filmy window, imagining grizzly bear dramas in my field of view. After quite some time, I was still looking at the same litter of bones and chew toys in the yard, the same gray jays and Steller's jays alighting among the debris to pick at smaller objects. We couldn't whisper or move around much in the little hut for fear of giving away our position. I found myself acutely conscious of the petroleum aromas permeating everything in the place. It was beginning to feel stifling.

Manley had long since given me his job summary: countless hours of driving, talking, and waiting, relieved by occasional seconds of drama. Any one of those bursts could change a person's life, just as it could conceivably alter the outcome of a species' struggle for survival. Still, I thought, it would be hard to muster the levels of patience required of a grizzly bear educator. But then I had only met Stahr in offhand fashion, really. To me, she was mostly a disembodied stream of electronic chirps. For the team, she was an individual whose fur they had held in their hands. That made all kinds of difference. They knew Stahr intimately by her appearance, her character, and her unique background, which they had pieced together. And they were acutely aware of how close their old acquaintance stood to being terminated if she screwed up much more.

That morning, Stahr's strategy, whatever it was, seemed to be playing out better than ours. Her signal was becoming more variable and weakening at times. She was on the move in the timber, probably in the opposite direction. Manley and Hunt finally called off the ambush. We packed up and bumped back along the North Fork road to the main Flathead Valley and on to Ferndale. It occurred to me that I still didn't know the bears there very well either, not in any personal way.

That was about to change.

ODE TO FRESH SIGN

Mᴏʀᴇ ᴛʜᴀɴ ᴀ ᴅᴇᴄᴀᴅᴇ ᴀɢᴏ, Gary Snyder, the fine and generous poet, sent me a signed limited-edition print of the following work.

Right in the Trail

Here it is, near the house,
A big pile, fat scats,
Studded with those deep red
Smooth-skinned manzanita berries,
Such a pile! Such droppings,
Awesome. And I saw how
The young girl in the story,
Had good cause to comment
On the bearscats she found while
Picking blueberries with her friends.
She laughed at them
Or maybe with them, jumped over them
(Bad luck!), and is reported
To have said "wide anus!"
To amuse or annoy the Big Brown Ones
Who are listening, of course.

They say the ladies
Have always gone berrying
And they all join together

To go out for the herring spawn,
Or to clean green salmon.
And that big set of lessons
On what bears really want,
Was brought back by the girl
Who made those comments:
She was taken on a year-long excursion
Back up in the mountains,
Through the tangled deadfalls,
Down into the den.
She had some pretty children by a
Young and handsome Bear.

Now I'm on the dirt
Looking at these scats
And I want to cry not knowing why
At the honor and the humor
Of coming on this sign
That is not found in books
Or transmitted in letters,
And is for women just as much as men,
A shining message for all species,
A glimpse at the Trace
Of the Great One's passing,
With a peek into her whole wild system—
And what was going on last week,
(Mostly still manzanita)—

Dear Bear: do stay around. Be good.
And though I know
It won't help to say this,

Chew your food.

FEEDING FERNIE

"Find the bear, Cassie," Carrie Hunt said to her favorite dog. "Find it. Show us the bear." There was no bear at the moment. Hunt was just having her dogs find the routes that Fernie and her two cubs used to enter and leave the yard of an unoccupied house not far from Ferndale. Cassie's nose revealed trails leading between the homesite and the willow brush lining a bend of the Swan River close by on the east. The big male dog, Rio, led the way to a couple of exploratory diggings along the bears' routes, then pulled me back toward the house and began sniffing piles of moderately processed apples. They were grizz dung. Scattered among autumn-loosed leaves and broken-off twigs, the stuff looked like pie filling and smelled like funky cider; and underneath the old apple trees at the heart of the yard, it lay thick as horse droppings in a busy corral.

Most of the sign was days old. To break a pattern of repeated nighttime raids here by the famished grizzly trio, Manley and Hunt had picked what remained of the apple crop and some nearby plums and removed them from the property. It looked as though the grizzlies had returned once or twice since to reconnoiter but had departed in fairly short order. We circled the house, inspecting it, as the bears must have done. Several cracked branches still attached to a chokecherry tree draped earthward at odd angles, but the building was neat as a pin. Neither we nor the dogs could find a scratch on it.

"GOOOOD girl, Cassie! Thank you, Rio!" Hunt cheered, handing out kibble treats all around. That the bears had more or less lost interest in the place was important to know. More than that, it was crucial, because the bear team was once again steering grizzly bear management in unprecedented directions. At the same time they were defruiting this yard, they were practicing something that would have got them fined and kicked out of any national park in the country. They were violating all kinds of rules against habituating bears to food near human settlement. They were doing what they had spent so many hours, season after season, pleading with residents never to do. The bear teachers were feeding the bears.

"You're bad people," I told Manley.

"Okay, I'll tell you how we're going about this," he said, and pointed toward the river. "We noticed Fernie and the cubs spending a lot of time in that patch of woods. They'd found a safe spot, or as safe a spot as they're going to come on in the middle of a developed area. They'd been sticking to it pretty tight during the day, so no one could see them, and feeding mostly at night. We called the owners and got their permission to let the bears stay there, and we went out and started picking up some deer carcasses." (The state highway patrol and county road crews keep the wildlife department informed about roadkills. Normally, the meat is distributed to the local food bank if salvageable, and used for bait if not.) "We hauled three dead deer out to that woodlot and dumped them in a pile, and we're just going to let the bears hole up there and eat on them a while."

I asked, "What happened to educating grizzlies?"

"The question for now is, would we rather have them settle in there and put on some weight or keep wandering back and forth from property to property?" Hunt responded. "We'll still do deterrence if it's called for, but I'm not sure how much you can teach a grizzly when it doesn't have any options left, you know? You can't fight the conditions in a year like this. That mother bear is going to stay around until she gets enough food one way or the other. She might as well get it from us. We have permission to try this supplemental feeding experiment for a week. We got hold of every neighbor we could find and told them what we're doing, and nobody really objected. When the bears have something in their stomachs, okay, we can go back to work on them. I'm hoping we won't have to. If they can fatten up enough, they ought to be primed to leave for the mountains and den."

From an open vantage point, I looked across the river at the trees that hid the cache of donated groceries and three grizzly bears on welfare. The setting was surrounded by houses, fields, and pastures. A new subdivision called Bear Meadows stretched away toward the east not far from an airstrip for small planes. Automobiles drew dust curtains along the grid of dirt roads, and a paved highway ran along the base of the Swan Mountains. Above stood Mount Aeneas, Three Eagles, and the other peaks of the range, massive repositories of solitude and tranquility, shining with promise. They were no more than six to eight miles from the bear family. They might as well have been dozens. For want of a square meal, Fernie had forsaken those mountains and was existing as a sort of suburban guerilla. The team was still trying to come up with a strategy to ensure that her choice wouldn't prove fatal.

Our patrol of the yard with the apple trees took place in early October. From that afternoon on, we were bouncing between Ferndale and Bigfork grizzlies, North Fork grizzlies, a male filching barnyard fowl from a clearing in the woods northeast of the Flathead Valley, and an assortment of other silvertips. Every so often, I would head home for a few hours to do things like sleep and talk about a subject other than *Ursus arctos horribilis.*

One morning, I grabbed my coffee and jumped into the bear team's pickup to revisit the meadow with the chicken-thieving grizz. Manley and Bryan Benn, a volunteer from a grizzly bear research and conservation group in Alberta, had left a baited culvert trap at the clearing's far end. The big steel cylinder stood untouched. Back toward the main house, we inspected the electric fencing that the team had installed around the chicken coops. This too was undisturbed, still ready to make a grizzly jump. So were the "critter gitters," or bear scarers—sonic alarms triggered when an infrared beam is broken—that Manley had nailed to the building. After a chat to reassure the landowner that the raider seemed to have found other interests, we left. Hunt joined us in the main valley, and we headed south toward Flathead Lake. We were still a couple of miles from where Fernie and the cubs had been hunkered down over their donated deer meat when Manley, fiddling with the radio receiver, muttered, "Uh-oh. Here we go."

You might say that the supplemental feeding worked, and that it didn't. Hunt and Manley had provisioned the bears with several hundred pounds of carcasses. The expectation was that this would hold a 250-pound female and two 50-pound cubs in the woodlot for some time. Yet within a few days, as Manley admiringly noted later, "she and the cubs slicked it all up." Of course, the bears would have had help from coyotes, skunks, ravens, magpies, and other scavengers, and some of the deer weight was inedible hide and bone. It was nonetheless an impressive bit of dining. My guess was that Fernie no longer weighed less than the beefy guy who had sold us gas that day. I might soon have a chance to see for myself, for Fernie and her offspring were out and about again, roaming a densely populated rural suburb known as Swan Hill.

If you mark the direction from which a signal comes in best, then move some distance and take a second reading, the animal wearing the transmitter will be found roughly where the two lines of direction intersect. The procedure, called triangulation, is simple. But signals reflect off hillsides, swirl around in minor Bermuda Triangles of electromagnetic weirdness, and get blocked altogether by gullies, thick timber, buildings, and the like. Unless you are tracking from an airplane, getting a good, clean fix on a collared bear is almost always a more drawn-out task than you would like it to be.

Fernie's signal told us only that she was somewhere toward the upper portion of Swan Hill and angling down its eastern face. Her exact location was a moot point anyway, because she was traveling fast. We drove to a home we reckoned might be in her path, an Old World–style cottage with ornate trim and a neatly landscaped yard that boasted bird feeders out front. Hunt and Manley looked at each other and, without a word, got out of the truck to go knock on the door and talk to the owners.

Sure enough, the couple we met had grizz tales to tell, chronicles of nighttime rustlings and shaggy shadows in the yard. The grizzly's image is so bound up with fangs, claws, blood, guts, and raw red meat that people cannot seem to put that together with the snitching of snacks set out for chickadees. These two folks were plumb mystified. They needed a crash course in big bear realities, and Hunt was just the person to deliver it. She's a rapid-fire, cook-everything-on-high, pull-out-the-stops evangelist on the subject. People respond because they recognize that she possesses a store of intimate knowledge about a creature they know mostly from rumors and reheated tales, and she is absolutely sincere.

As her examples and stories of grizzly instruction spill forth, people also infer, correctly, that this woman is fearless. On top of that, she arrives with a pack of wonderful looking, somewhat aloof, businesslike dogs that most folks have never seen before, which seldom fails to bolster the impression that something special is going on. And she has this partner from the Department of Fish, Wildlife & Parks.

Dressed like the game warden who politely checks your catch of trout and, as long as you're under your limit, lets you know where they're getting all the big ones, Manley is Montana born and bred, an aw-shucks, steady type who kicks the dust with a boot but looks you straight in the eye when he speaks. For many locals, he validates the whole dicey enterprise. He takes Hunt's expositions on bear training and grounds them in friendly advice and a detailed recounting of who the grizzly in the area is and what it has done to date. There is no hint in him of the rural West's favorite bogeyman—the rule-worshipping bureaucrat who acts too busy and important to seriously consider some yokel's concerns. Like Hunt, Manley will talk with you until you are talked out. Chances are, he already knows one or two of your neighbors from his years covering the countryside to keep on top of problem bears.

Manley did indeed have acquaintances in common with the couple living in the quasi-Bavarian cottage. In the space of a few minutes of watching the bear team work humans, I found myself thinking that the combination of Tim Manley and Carrie Hunt may be the best public relations service any grizzly ever had.

Fernie's signal, when we picked it up again, continued moving downhill. We followed, stopping at several more homes along the way to spread the word: Howdy. Say, there's a mother grizzly with two babies in your neighborhood. We don't consider her an aggressive bear, and we're working on herding her back toward the mountains. We just thought you would want to know. By the way, it would be great if you'd bring in the garbage can over there, and . . . you know, that old cowhide you've got draped over the fence by the corner should probably go somewhere out of reach too.

So far, Fernie had been interested in livestock feed, not livestock. But when we came to the home with a crowd of ostriches in an adjoining corral, nobody knew how to advise the owners other than to keep a sharp eye out and put the number for the bear team's mobile phone in a handy place. Like every other family we had met that day, this one was interested in the grizzly project and eager for particulars about the momma bear and her little ones. In people's eyes, I saw less hidden fear than genuine empathy and often a touch of pride. You live in Montana, where people are always talking about grizzlies. Maybe you've never seen one up close, but now you've got three running around next door. That just gave you some bragging rights. If nothing else, it's something to write friends back East about, to pass along as news at work the next day.

While the family queried Manley and Hunt about wrangling grizz, I wanted to know more about raising desert-dwelling birds in northern Montana, where winter temperatures sometimes crack forty below zero. But my amazement paled next to that of a team member who had switched from another crew's truck to ours and now stood with me by the ostrich pen. His name was Kai-Eerik Nyholm. From Finland, he was an authority on the habits of large northern wildlife, but I'm not sure he had been eye to eye before with a bird taller than he was.

Nyholm had come to learn how the Partners in Life program operated day to day. He needed to decide whether this approach to bear conditioning might be applicable in his home country. The irony was that Finns invented Karelian bear dogs. (Their neighbors in northwestern Russia make the same claim about the breed, which is relatively recent, recognized only in the 1930s.) The Nyholm family had tutored Hunt on how to choose and train Karelians when she was in Finland gathering information for two months. Kai-Eerik's father was one of the country's leading brown bear experts. From early childhood, the son had been using Karelians to chase down big game such as European moose as well as bears. He also grew up with a brown bear orphaned by hunters.

As we left the ostriches and zigzagged down the road network toward the base of Swan Hill, where Fernie seemed bound, I learned that the orphan's name was Vyoti—"'White Collar' in Finnish," Nyholm said. "He made best friends with one of the puppies we raised with him, and he is very intelligent. The door of our farmhouse has a latch that works by pulling a string. After two tries, Vyoti discovered how to pull it open while he wedged his rump in the door to keep it from closing. We took him with us when we went ice fishing once. We showed the bear that all trout and whitefish are ours. Different kinds like perch, he could have. This bear would begin to dance when he saw those other types of fish coming up through the ice hole. I was very amazed by the animal's ability to learn so quickly. Today, Vyoti weighs about 300 kilos. You can understand why he is no longer living with us in the house."

Ahead of us but still out of view, Fernie had just trotted past a cluster of dwellings. They included a day care center, a home with kids' tricycles in the yard, and a little brown box of a house from whose porch a woman with a kindergarten-age child was hailing us. I suspected we were about to get an earful about rampant grizzlies and arrogant wildlife officials, but she said neighbors already had a phone tree going and she knew about Fernie's itinerant family. Her comment was, "Cool. Maybe we'll get to see them." Like many residents, she was aware of what sort of year the grizzlies were having. So many black bears facing the same food shortages had poured out of the hills that drivers were slamming into them all over the Flathead Valley. The toll from automobiles was approaching several dozen.

If a solitary grizzly had been regularly showing itself three times as far away from only one-tenth as many people in Glacier Park, rangers would have been patrolling the area, closing trails, and stapling up their warning signs, which depict a lean, ornery looking grizzly on a bright orange background with the proclamation DANGER! By comparison, what was happening around Swan Hill was a bet on a bronc ride. It seemed amazing that authorities were willing to let the team try dealing with a silvertip this way, amazing that people were so understanding. And it was revolutionary when compared to earlier years, when grizzlies had official protection as a threatened species but were always removed and often terminated in circumstances like these. I wondered if the level of tolerance I was witnessing might not be the long-missing ingredient necessary for a true recovery.

Nyholm told me that Finland had about 800 brown bears, very similar to the number estimated for the lower forty-eight states in 1975, when the grizzly was listed. But the tolerance on display around us was missing in his country. Legal hunting, poaching, and execution for crop and livestock depredation were removing close to 100 brown bears there every year. "This is too high to be sustained," he told me. "It is why we must look into trying something like aversive conditioning with the help of the dogs."

For the moment, I was less than certain about what conditioning had accomplished in Fernie's case. We had followed her signal north along the river to yet another set of alerted homeowners and were now trying to catch sight of her in the Swan Horseshoe subdivision area, where she had been captured earlier that fall. At the same time, I realized how closely we had been trailing this family without being able to spot them. No matter how developed a locale, Fernie unerringly picked her way through it via the last intimations of wildness—the woodlots and groves, the little bogs and brushy bottoms, the windbreaks and hedgerows, even the ditches with tall weeds.

Although the patterns we saw might have been partly a tribute to natural tendencies on the part of a smallish, subordinate female, grizzlies are not creatures of hidey-holes and leafy tangles. They like their open spaces. Avoiding those, becoming more active at night, and behaving surreptitiously in general are learned traits. Fernie's education was showing. Maybe the appropriate thing to ask was how much the team had actually taught her and how much she had taught herself. Then again, in light of the human education going on from one neighborhood to the next as the team moved through, yakking and kibbitzing and leaving Montana cleaner than they found it, maybe the education of grizzlies was secondary. Habituating people to living near great bears has been the greatest challenge all along.

One older woman in the subdivision had lived there sixteen years and had never seen a bear of any kind, and that was fine by her. Two nights before we arrived, she'd heard rustlings in the yard. Her husband had built several bird feeders there. In fact, he'd constructed platforms almost large enough for a person to sleep on, and the couple kept them filled with at least a hundred pounds of sunflower seeds and millet. They spread more seeds atop the firewood stacked high on the back porch. That way, they could watch birds close-up from the dining room. The next night was quieter, but at a quarter after five that morning, the woman had awakened to the sight of two little grizzlies clambering over the woodpile, licking up birdseed, and their mother nearby at the feeders.

For the next forty-five minutes, the woman crouched behind a couch gripping a .357 magnum pistol, peeping up at Fernie's cubs as they romped and gobbled atop the firewood stacks. Her husband was away working somewhere. She called the sheriff, and she called her daughter, who lived close by. The daughter sent her own husband over with a shotgun. By the time the man arrived, the bear family had vanished. The older woman stayed huddled inside her house the rest of the morning, and she didn't look very comfortable when she came out in the yard to tell her story. Though surrounded by the bear crew and dogs, she kept casting wary glances over our shoulders in the direction of the river brush.

The woman's daughter showed up. In talking with her, we found out that Fernie's family hadn't been as safely ensconced in the woodlot with the deer carcasses as we assumed. They had been at a neighbor's bird feeder three nights ago, she said. In other words, in between gobbling their weight in meat, they had still gone raiding. Good lord, I marveled, what creatures! What appetites! What welfare chiselers!

Manley and Hunt took turns speaking to the women and cleaning out the bird feeders. I helped scoop, rake, and lug. As I was whisking more pounds of little damn millet seeds off the woodpile, log by log, crack by crack, I thought that this was a funny way to resurrect grizzly bears. It wasn't anything like what I had had in mind when I hooked up with the team. Neither was pulling over on highways to load up ripe roadkills for bait so often that I acquired the bear teachers' habit of keeping one eye cocked for flocks of magpies and ravens. Nor could this could have been farther from the television version—a wildlife special about sharing a day in the life of the continent's most powerful predator. But it had to be done.

Meanwhile, Hunt and Manley agreed, the time had come for Fernie to look toward the mountains and get gone. Manley, Bryan Benn the Canadian, and Kai-Eerik Nyholm the Finn made a scent trail in that direction by dragging a fresh deer carcass behind a truck with a rope. At intervals, they chucked out tidbits of meat to be sure that the bears' interest would not flag en route. The trail ended about a mile east in another copse. Manley left the carcass there as a reward. He needed something to hold the grizzlies long enough for the team to drag the next segment on what he hoped would be a continuous journey eastward.

Before long, Fernie appeared a couple hundred yards away from the house with the jumbo bird feeders as if conjured from the riverbank's dark brown shrub stems and tall golden grasses. Knowing the grizzly was somewhere in that ribbon of brush, Manley had started the drag trail parallel to it so that she could easily get onto the scent. She did. I thought I had briefly spied her other days, a shoulder showing here through the boughs, a silvery length of flank disappearing there over a hill. Once after dark, I'd caught her bulky shape in the distance while surveying with a night vision scope, or else I'd seen some other animal and let my imagination fill in. Now here came the famous Fernie, close and in full view at last. She was walking rapidly but stopped long enough to down each meat scrap along the way. From time to time, she also paused to turn partway around and check on the progress of her cubs, which some of the crew had begun calling Nip and Tuck.

Fernie was a modest-size grizz, all right—I'd seen bigger black bears and taller deer—but she looked bulky enough in her autumn coat. While one cub remained distinctly smaller than the other, they both looked reasonably round too. As they loped to catch up with their mother, they shoved and tugged at each other as cubs with normal stores of bumbling energy will. There was nothing exceptional about any of these animals, and that was good in the sense that they had all been noticeably on the slim side before.

No, nothing extraordinary about them, except that they were grizzlies, and they were walking around like they had just bought themselves a little riverside acreage and planned to share the Montana dream down here in the lowlands. The word that came to mind was not awesome but presumptuous. Mischievous. Canny. Moments later, they evaporated into the brush again.

Patient as always, the team chose to settle in and see what the bear family was going to do rather than force the issue. Fernie knew about the scent trail now. It was up to her to decide how and when to follow it farther. If she felt threatened, her urge to get clear would override the drive for food—especially now that she was better nourished—and the plan to lure her eastward in stages would be bollixed.

We waited a while in the trucks in case Fernie popped back in view. When she didn't, we withdrew to give her more space. The older woman's daughter arranged for us to hang out inside an untenanted house that she and her husband had just finished building across the subdivision's meadow. We would have had grizzly viewing from the sofa on white wall-to-wall carpeting. If Fernie had shown up. Our guess was that she was waiting for dusk to make her move back onto the scent trail. But the hours passed, and dusk failed to bring her out. Her signal shifted somewhat in the direction that the scent trail led. We moved over to the house closest to Fernie's new location to check the grounds for possible attractants and to be sure the owners had not somehow missed hearing about their grizzly bear neighbors.

The people inside were named Mickie and John, and we no sooner introduced ourselves than they invited us to join them in a pleasantly bright, well-appointed new kitchen and handed around coffee and pastrami on rye. We were grateful just for the warmth of the room. A clear-sky night had brought frosty temperatures quickly after sunset. Mickie pressed up against the sliding glass doors, hoping for a glimpse of the bears. Manley and Hunt traded places talking at the table and stepping outside to take readings with the radio receiver. I sipped a soft drink and watched sports on television, thinking that things were definitely looking up for the nighttime shift on the grizzly stakeout.

When Manley's mobile phone beeped, I knew the soft life was probably coming to an end. He rarely receives a call telling him that everything is going along wonderfully. This fall, at this hour, there was virtually no chance that he would not end up listening to a complaint about a bear. I tried to remind myself that for every trouble-maker we heard about, others down in the same stretch of country were keeping acceptably low profiles, in several cases because the team had conditioned them to do so. And at least a couple hundred more grizzlies were staying out of sight and out of mind in the back-country. Whatever the right combination was—of home range location, microclimates for plant growth, social rank, a strong aversion to humans, plain luck, or factors we weren't aware of—they had enough of it to get by, while others didn't.

Manley was nodding and saying yes, um-hmm, I see, then pinching his lips in resignation when he looked over at us. The call was from a woman named Deb, who with her husband, Dan, owned and operated the Polebridge Mercantile Store near the North Fork. She wanted the team to know that earlier in the day a real estate agent had taken clients to look over a cabin and property up Red Meadow Creek, half a dozen miles north of Polebridge. The first thing they noticed as they drove in was a grizzly tearing the door off the storage shed. This was not conducive to generating interest on the part of prospective home buyers. The people had stopped in at the store to tell their story, and Deb felt she should inform Manley. Oh, and the ex-clients said the grizzly had a cub with her.

"*A* cub?" I heard Manley ask.

The answer was affirmative. One cub. Manley shook his head. "Stahr," he said.

NEIGHBORS AND OUTLAWS

WHY ARE YOU SPENDING so much time and money on one bear?' I get that question all the time," Tim Manley sighed. "My answer is, 'Because we're at a point where a single bear, especially a breeding female, might make the difference between a population that's gradually recovering and one that's headed downhill. That's why.'" In practice, he, Carrie Hunt, and their assistants seldom had the luxury of concentrating on any one grizzly to the exclusion of others for very long.

In the Flathead Valley proper, the team was dealing not only with Fernie but with Sully, a male that, like her, hailed from the South Fork of the Flathead River; Crusty, a big older male that had followed the joined flows of the South Fork and Middle Fork downstream to the outskirts of the town of Columbia Falls; Olsen's male, a grizz wandering near Echo Lake on the valley's eastern side; and Easy, a female that had taken up ambling through the town of Whitefish, where I was currently living. Meanwhile, they had to keep up with the chicken-eating male northwest of Whitefish near the little logging mill town of Olney and with a female in the same general vicinity.

Along with Stahr, Louie, Daryl, and her sibling, Blade, the North Fork held troublemakers known as B.C., a male whose initials stood for Big Creek; No. 47, a twenty-nine-year-old male first captured during a Canadian research project in the North Fork's headwaters and now looting human supplies a few miles south of the international line; and four grizzlies—one male and a female with two cubs—coming down out of the Apgar Range near the southern end of this Flathead tributary.

Calls also came in now and then about grizz unfamiliar to the team. Not having a name meant a bear hadn't been in trouble enough to earn one. These were the ideal animals to work with. Catch one in the wrong place once or twice—HEY BEAR! BOOM! KA-POW! BARK BARK BARK! KA-POW! HEY BEAR! BOOM!—and it may decide that whatever the attraction was, is not worth the pandemonium, and resume life in the wild determined to avoid people. Most bears with names had already learned too much about human food to be scared straight that easily. As Manley had made clear earlier, the team didn't expect to be able to turn all these animals around. They knew some would be killed. But they knew with equal certainty that only a few years before, virtually every bear causing real problems would have ended up dead.

~ ~ ~

Throughout the first part of the twentieth century, grizzlies in Glacier and Yellowstone National Parks had been allowed to panhandle and loot garbage. Officials accepted this within limits as entertainment for visitors. Why not? Fatal incidents had been as rare as solar eclipses. For a while, Yellowstone staff went so far as to set up bleacher seats around an open dump. The boomer generation grew up with the cartoon television characters Yogi Bear and his sidekick, Boo-Boo, whose lives in Jellystone Park were devoted to hornswoggling tourists out of picnic lunches, and the premise didn't seem all that far off the mark.

Grizzlies were drawn to artificial food beyond the parks as well. Some tourist-store and lodge owners in neighboring communities purposefully left garbage bins open to attract grizzlies, whose nightly Dumpster-diving show was good for business. But having no legal protection outside parks prior to 1975, most of those bears eventually died of lead poisoning, as the saying goes, meaning lead in the form of bullets.

During the 1960s and 1970s, a series of attacks in park camp-grounds by grizzlies conditioned to non-natural food left several people dead. The killings were ghastly, and the media sensationalized them to the hilt. The public was in shock. Wildlife officials were in hot water. They completely reversed course. In short order, the gospel became that any grizzly in or out of a park that loses its fear of humans poses a deadly threat and has to be treated as such—in short, disposed of.

The team was out to prove differently. To do so required putting up their own lives and those of the public as collateral, along with the credibility of wildlife agencies. It would be hard to find a dicier experiment in the field of conservation. Yet, is there a more generous, optimistic expression of the commitment to preserve species than taking the trouble to teach a huge, long-clawed one how to live with us? However mundane our tooling around the county in trucks and picking up refuse and other potential attractants might seem on the surface, something extraordinary was afoot here. At least, that was my explanation for why I found myself gazing with pride upon a leaky gallon jar of pickles, a tossed-out bunch of overripe bananas, and a forgotten garbage sack—our haul from the first three properties we visited one morning.

— — —

We searched for Stahr around the cabin whose storage shed she had reportedly been tearing into when the real estate agent took two prospective buyers to look over the place. Following up on the story, the team learned that the door was already askew when the salesman arrived. Noticing a cub at the doorway, he had told his clients, "Um, you might want to just wait here a moment." At which point the grizzly mother had emerged from the building.

The door was hanging loose still. We fixed it. The main task at hand proved to be cleaning out the moldering bags of dog food and grain inside that had inspired the grizzly to pry loose the door in the first place. The chore was made more interesting by the fact that Stahr could probably hear and smell us shoving aside junk and scooping up the damp mash of crumbs mixed with mouse turds.

When we had first arrived, she had made an appearance in the yard with her cub and a lighter colored, nearly grown bear. It was her older offspring, Louie. Born in 1995 and on his own since the summer of 1997, he was the one discovered to be trailing Stahr from time to time as a subadult. Now in his fourth year of life, this male had met up with mom and was apparently being tolerated at close quarters despite the presence of an offspring from the current year. It was news to the team, since Louie's radio had given out. Such a reunion was also news in terms of what was known of grizzly social behavior. No one was sure what to make of it, though, because the animals' foraging activities had strayed so far from natural patterns.

Once the three bears became aware of us, they went out of view. But according to Stahr's signal, they didn't go far. Accidentally walking up on them as we made rounds of the yard remained a possibility. It not a large worry, though, and the chances were still slimmer that the bears would come in closer, now that they knew we were here. On the other hand, there was always the chance that one of these grizzlies was about to change its habit of avoiding confrontations.

You can't afford to wear yourself out being hyperalert when you're on call around the clock. Besides, it's not cool to act rattled around professional bear people. But with a grizzly anywhere nearby, you don't want to overdo the casual pose. Trying to convince yourself that the bear *won't* come freight-training over and turn you into a minced shadow of your former self has zero survival value. I suppose it's a blessing that you wouldn't have time to think about what a fool you were.

If I find myself starting to take a grizzly for granted, no matter how shy, disinterested, or ooh-snoogie-woogums it might be acting at the time, I try to recall one of two scenes. The first is Alaska's McNeil River in July, as the king salmon (chinook) run was winding down and humpback salmon (pinks) began leaping upstream in their place. I was standing on the bank next to ten other people and fifty-six coastal grizzlies, the farthest of which were about 150 yards distant and the closest barely 10 feet. Oddly, the fact that so many brown bears were paying us no real heed made me as unconcerned as I had ever been in the animals' presence.

Two of the biggest ones were roughhousing nearby, a common enough activity. I don't know what kindled the change—a missed cue, a violation of play-fighting rules, a previous grievance coming to the fore?—but with a roar, one 900-pound grizzly picked up the other by the neck with its teeth and tossed the giant opponent over its back. The tossee rolled and plunged away raising fountains of spray. That was it. The action lasted maybe two seconds. By the time the surprise wore off and I looked around, the nearest bears were all fishing again, as though I had only daydreamed of a colossal grizz flying upside down.

The second scene is a high meadow colored with Indian paintbrush, gentians, avalanche lilies, and a good-size blondish grizzly bear. A Columbian ground squirrel came out of its burrow and scurried several feet uphill as I peered from behind a line of stunted spruce. When the rodent stood up on its hindquarters for a look around, it and the bear saw each other at the same time, and the chase was on. As big game dramas go, this wasn't much. It was the grizzly's agility that stunned me. The muscle-bound hulk matched the ground squirrel's every feint and turn, braked and reversed directions like a soccer star, spun in place, zigzagged ahead, slammed down a paw, and had itself a ground squirrel hors d'oeuvre. Just . . . like . . . THAT.

Either recollection serves, because it always arrives with other memory fragments trailing behind—of grizzlies delivering blows shiver-quick, overturning ponderous boulders with wrist flicks while searching for insects, whirling in a blur upon hearing a pinecone fall or a jay screech behind them, going from a standstill to a racehorse gallop in a heart squeeze, and on and on. Whatever you think a grizzly is capable of, I tell myself, you'd better think harder. No shortcuts. No I'm-sending-out-vibes-of-mellowness-to-this-bear. Stay sharp or leave.

Or go the shark cage route. There was a corral near the shed, and a metal horse trailer was parked between the corral fence and the building. Realizing that we had the perfect close-up blind for observation, Ted Woods, the *Smithsonian* photographer, and I made plans to enter the trailer that evening. Hunt and Manley would shut us in and retire to the pickup truck, waiting to ambush Stahr if she returned. After nightfall, we took up positions. The forest grew so quiet that the sound of my jacket fabric rubbing as I shifted around inside the trailer seemed earsplitting. Woods had to shush me more than once.

Patience is part of the wildlife photographer's trade, as it is with bear teachers. I tried to emulate Woods. We sat like corpses and let the October chill seep into our bones uncontested. For lack of distractions, I found myself studying the trailer for weaknesses and recalling the ease with which captive grizzlies I'd met pushed up bars and worked latches to open doors. The crackle of our two-way radio in the darkness made me jump. Hunt was on the air, whispering something about leaving. The next thing we heard was her and Manley starting up the truck and bumping away down the track. When they had gone, the forest really grew quiet.

Slowly going hypothermic in a pitch-black horse trailer in the backwoods waiting for grizzlies to come by didn't make a great deal of sense. At the same time, it struck me as a strange kind of privilege—or it would be if any bears approached. None did. I finally had to stand up and move to get warm blood into my hands and feet. I was pacing tiptoe style, setting each foot down carefully as a jewel thief, when we heard the grizzlies.

In between the rustling of their footfalls, we noticed Stahr making soft chuffs and growls. The cub grumbled, bleated, and mewled. It was like listening in on a private conversation. Not to make too much of it—the little one may have been whining for a sip of milk while mother said forget it—but the continual communication made me intensely curious. How often are grizzlies talking to each other out of range of our hearing? How varied might the messages be that pass between mother and young?

The night was pitch black. We could scarcely discern the animals' outlines, and they were only about fifteen feet away. Woods produced the night vision scope Manley had lent us. When I put it to my eye, the field of view was all grizzly bear—luminous, twinkling, pale green grizz, due to the optical effects of the photomultiplying device. Even in that hue, Stahr's coat looked streaked and frosted with silver.

The mother and baby kept close together and touched faces from time to time. Stahr was slightly bigger than I had previously realized. The surviving cub seemed smaller. They entered the shed tentatively and stayed only a short while before galloping off, going "whuff-whuff-whuff." Either they detected us, or they heard Hunt and Manley approaching in the truck from down the road a ways. Woods fired off a couple of flash pictures in the process, so the pair got at least a small dose of aversive conditioning.

The team set out a culvert trap at the property. Stahr avoided it, but on the 17th of October, Louie went in. He was given a new radio collar and released on site. Stahr continued to prospect around homes where she had previously found food. One place she didn't raid again was Flo's. The team had cajoled the woman into letting them haul all her dog food from the house and porch into the barn-garage. They then enclosed the building with electric fencing and tacked up critter gitters, the sonic bear scarers, and that was the end of Flo's grizzly problems.

— ~ —

At the beginning of the last week of October, a grizzly was struck by a train along the Flathead's Middle Fork. Manley and Kai-Eerik Nyholm used the Karelians to track the bear. They found it lying in some brush. It was a female, four years old and about 300 pounds. She was paralyzed. They had to finish her off. This east-west railroad is a line less than ten feet wide within thousands of square miles of habitat. Yet it kills grizzlies every year because the container cars rattling down the line spill grain. Small amounts attract elk and deer, which get smacked on the tracks, and their carcasses lure grizzlies. Larger grain spills draw grizzlies directly. Near the four-year-old female, the Karelians sniffed out fresh droppings. They contained sunflower seeds from someone's bird feeder.

Later in the week, we rolled toward the North Fork again and stopped to coffee up at the Polebridge Mercantile. Known to locals as the Merc, the store is a false-front Old West structure built at the start of the last century. The walls are festooned with antiques from rusty traps to two-man whipsaws, along with the obligatory elk antlers. This is a place where you can resupply with beans and beer, leave notes for companions, buy locally made curios, or just hang around the woodstove and warm up, maybe find someone to talk with if you've been solo in your cabin a while.

When my wife, Karen, and I were living full-time along the North Fork, we had food on the table only because the Merc's previous owners, Karen Feather and John Gray, let us slide by on credit all winter. When I skied in once to buy several boxes of wooden matches, Feather told me to forget it; she had to charge too much for items like that. "I'll buy you some wholesale on my supply run to town tomorrow," she told me. "You can pick them up and pay me back when you come to get mail." It was that kind of store.

As the valley's informal communications hub, the Merc is also a good place to catch up on scuttlebutt about North Fork grizz that might not have reached official ears. Some locals are reluctant to call the wildlife department about bear problems, either because they don't consider a little mooching to be serious, they have their own solution in mind (the triple-S technique—shoot, shovel, and shut up—being a perennial favorite), they don't much like government authorities in general, or they like grizzlies and worry that some official will come to trap or kill them. Now and then the Merc has grizzly stories of its own. Earlier that year, for instance, the current owners, the Kaufmanns, had loaded a truck with garbage for a trip to town, and Stahr had climbed into it before they pulled out.

By 9:00 A.M., we had checked on Daryl, Blade, and a yet-to-be-named grizz the team had worked—"*Still* being good," Hunt declared with satisfaction—and had used three dogs and two cracker shell rounds to chase Stahr off the benchland that held the photographer's cabin. Several other cabins, all unoccupied, shared that foothill plateau. Stahr's muddy paw prints stood out on one of them like rustic designs. They brought to mind the marks that my wife and I had found on our North Fork cabin windows before we understood that having a compost pile for the garden was not a sound idea on the edge of Glacier Park. Another set of grizz prints appeared a couple of years later on the front door. I took these more as signs of curiosity than of any serious effort to break in.

As far as we knew, Stahr hadn't touched a claw to our cabin. But she had surely looked it over during her travels, for she had been seen around the nearest homes north and south. We'd found fresh spoor along the river channel and streams on our property that fall, but we did every fall. And during much of the summer and spring. Unlike the situation in the main Flathead Valley, there were always grizzlies in the North Fork bottomlands.

Most of the local residents were pretty good at minding their own business, and the same was true of most North Fork grizz. I lost count of how many times grizzlies made a point of avoiding Karen and me as we strolled in the riverside forests while living there. We heard them whuff-whuffing out of our way often enough. Coming back late from trips to town, we hiked in about a half mile to the cabin at all hours of the night to the sound of crashing in the brush nearby. More than once, I got home from the Northern Lights Saloon, a little log building situated next to the Merc, by staggering for two miles on game trails through the woods drunk and helpless as a man can be and still move. I am here to testify that North Fork grizzlies, on the whole, were decent neighbors. Taking into account their potential for mayhem, plus the fact that there are as at least as many per square mile in the greater North Fork area as in any other part of the contiguous states, they treated us more than graciously.

Here's the equation: In landscapes where human and grizzly ranges overlap, you have a given number of people and a given number of grizzlies making an effort to get along. Then you have a percentage of people unconsciously training a percentage of grizzlies to come for artificial food. Now factor in the bear team, working like crazy to change problem people's behavior and untrain problem bears. Responsive home owners, sensitive individual bears, and ones not yet addicted to handouts all raise the team's chances of success. An upper limit is set by the fact that certain people and certain bears act impervious to instruction for one set of reasons or another. Does the math work out to a recovery? Probably, assuming you can persuade just a few more folks to join in and you don't get poor natural food production for too many years in a row.

As for Stahr's part in this, she had pretty much turned outlaw. This was a grizzly now making few if any attempts at natural foraging in between cabin visits, and switching her modus operandi from nocturnal raids to bolder and bolder daylight probes. Other mother grizz had already dug their way into the dark earth instead, mid-October to mid-November being the usual time for females and immature bears to begin a long winter's nap. The team was merely trying to keep Stahr from causing more serious damage while praying that, any day now, she too might head up into the mountains to den.

"We got five [rubber bullet] hits on her one day around cabins and the road," Manley said. "But about all that's doing anymore is making her back off and go on to the next property where she has found food. Louie's been causing more trouble too. They're both beyond the guidelines. I've asked my boss whether the time had come to take them in [to be permanently caged or put down]. He said we've lost so many bears this year that he didn't think we could afford to lose any more. He told us to keep trying our best to hold the line, so that's what we're doing."

By late morning that same day, Stahr and her cub had traveled south off the benchland to Hay Creek and broken into a stash of trout pellets by the pond dug next to a cabin. She found garbage around the place as well. The owner said he thought all the grizzlies were asleep by now. As a result, Stahr won yet another food reward to counter the punishment we were doling out. We leashed onto the

EASY, a female who grew up on the slopes of Big Mountain at the southern end of the Whitefish Range and went on to become a frequent visitor to the lawns and local golf courses at lower elevations. [DEREK REICH]

LACY investigates a fruit tree *(above, left)* in the yard of a Whitefish home and *(above, right)* turns her attention to one of the most ubiquitous attractions. This bear became fairly expert at raiding birdseed, dog chow, and other food available in human territory. [DEREK REICH]

ARRESTED, Lacy awaits relocation to the backcountry. [DEREK REICH]

ON CALL, Carrie Hunt *(above)* informs a cabin owner that leaving dog food on her porch was an invitation to the grizzly that came by. *(Left)* Holding a portable antenna aloft, Tim Manley joins Hunt on the trail of a night-roaming grizz wearing a radio collar. The third member of the team, a Karelian bear dog, has just caught their quarry's scent. [Derek Reich]

STAHR visits an inhabited area of the North Fork with a surviving cub *(above; photo by Kai-Eerik Nyholm/Wind River Bear Institute)* in 1998 and is captured with her two new cubs *(left; photo by Derek Reich)* in 2000.

CARRIE HUNT, head of the Wind River Bear Institute, trains the Karelian known as Eilu, one of two bear dogs she imported from their native country of Finland to begin her novel experiment in educating bears. [DEREK REICH]

SHOWTIME for Karelians Kuma, Cassidy, Blaze, and Tuffy during a bear conflict presentation held at a ski resort. [DEREK REICH]

TANK, a movie-star grizz with scores of trained behaviors in his repertoire, relaxes at Wasatch Rocky Mountain Wildlife. The facility's owners acquire only bears born in captivity or orphaned in the wild. [DEREK REICH]

DAKOTA'S CUBS

are unable to move or even blink after being dosed with a muscle-immobilizing drug during a capture operation in the Stillwater Valley. The author inspects blindfolds placed over the young bears' eyes to protect them from light and dust until they begin to recover. [DEREK REICH]

DAKOTA will be reunited with her cubs, and all three will be released along the North Fork of the Flathead River next to Glacier National Park. [DEREK REICH]

A GRIZZLY commands attention merely by being in the same zip code. [Derek Reich]

dogs and chased her off. She was back a few minutes later. The team got some rubber bullets on her flanks, and the pair of grizzlies sprinted away. According to the mother's signal, she was on a course straight to the Stahr property, for which she had been named. We followed her there, cleaned up some bird seed in a feeder, and then trailed her back to the trout ponds and banged her away once more.

It appeared to me that Stahr was hungry enough, outlaw enough, or both to look upon aversive conditioning as the price of doing business. The team agreed. Hunt reiterated her point about the difficulty of teaching bears in a year that didn't provide them many options. I asked why the team didn't put out food to hold Stahr in a secure spot, as they had done with Fernie. The answer, paradoxically, was that Fernie had been in a much more suburban part of the Flathead. In the North Fork Valley, private acreage amounts to a scattered archipelago within a sea of national park, federal forest, and state forest lands. The public is free to roam that domain; after all, they own it. And they were roaming great guns everywhere west of the park now that hunting season had started. Grizzlies can be ferociously defensive of a meat cache, and the likelihood of a sportsman in the woods unknowingly crossing from public property into private grounds and surprising Stahr as she fed on a donated carcass was too high.

Moreover, Stahr was a different kind of bear than Fernie. The clues were subtle and tough to articulate, but most of the team had the sense that a person would be a lot better off suddenly coming upon Fernie. Stahr was bigger. And although she had not yet displayed overt aggression—she could easily have clobbered Flo during their surprise meeting on the porch—she had a bit more of an edge to her. Perhaps this was only another way of saying that Stahr was likely to react in general grizzly bear fashion, whereas Fernie was more timid and easily dominated.

By three in the afternoon, Stahr had returned to the trout pond, the team's guns were firing, and Karelians were going nuts. The mother and cub left again toward the Stahr property. En route, they visited two other cabins, which happened to be those closest to mine on the south. We drove her out of those yards, kept her away from the yard at the Stahr property, and then lost sight of her for a while. When Stahr reappeared, she was too close to the road. The team smacked her again to try to get her to withdraw. She did.

"Yesterday, we set Oso [a Karelian male] on her up at Reimer's cabin," Hunt said, referring to a place on the benchland north of the Merc. "I think yesterday and today are the most work we've ever done on her." I could tell that Hunt was trying to call up her characteristic enthusiasm, but it wasn't really there. This wasn't bear training. It was nonstop guarding of cabins against grizzlies with a serious food deficit. Everyone knew it, and everyone was running out of ideas other than praying that Stahr would den.

The Stahr property was less than three miles from mine, which made the owner another of my nearest neighbors by North Fork standards. For perspective on the relative danger the grizzly bear posed, I had the memory of Roy, the previous owner of the Stahr acreage, and the unexpected winter visit he got from two men and a woman. They had broken out of prison in Oklahoma and were on a cross-country run for Canada when they saw the North Fork road on a map. It looked like a remote, unguarded route. Somewhere on their way up the valley, they discovered that the last miles leading to the border were snowed in for the winter. They were cruising around drunk and high on pills when they pulled into Roy's yard.

It could have been anybody's place. The trio pushed their way into his trailer, roughed him up, and started sucking down his whiskey. At some point, they decided they were going to escape into Canada by riding Roy's horses through the high country, mountain-man style. They ordered him to get saddles and supplies ready. He told them they were idiots if they thought they could get through that snowbound country on horseback. They slit his throat.

Stahr had habituated to the cracker shells. She scarcely looked up any longer when they exploded overhead. When a rubber dumdum round pounded her flank, she would spurt a few feet and then drop back to a determined walk. She knew what she was supposed to do.

She always left, but she was damned if she was going to do it at a run. We'd had the pair in view off and on all day, and I had not once seen the cub suckle or pause to take a bite of natural food. It simply trotted behind its mother, small and lean and confused, and I imagined that if I were as close as I had been in the horse trailer, I would have heard continual whimpering. Pop!—BOOM! Another cracker round burst over the pair's heads. They moved a shade faster for another short distance. I could hardly stand to watch much longer.

In the middle of the night, we took up position south of the Stahr property on a spread called Home Ranch Bottom. In addition to running the only major cattle operation in the valley, the owner had a small store and rented out trailer space to loggers, tree stand thinners, hunters, and folks who just wanted to be away from town for a while. Stahr had visited on another night and been rewarded with a bloody deer hide. We set up between trailers, waiting for the next shot at her.

I jogged in place outside the pickup a while to get warm. Hunt joined me, muttering about the tribulations of this mother bear, the last of her triplets, and the bear assumed to be her previous cub, Louie, recently seen too close to buildings again farther north. "You know," she said, "if Louie or Stahr do have to die, maybe at least they will have spurred North Forkers to do a little more cleanup. They keep talking about making some sort of local ordinance about feeding wildlife. Maybe they'll finally put one in place. I mean, for every person who's been leaving out food, there are two or three around here right now who are pretty pissed about messy neighbors. That's progress in a way, I guess."

The last I saw of Stahr and the little cub, they were shadows within moonshadows across the North Fork road from the Home Ranch Bottom store. They were watching and waiting for an opportunity, just as we were. I wondered if the cub had ever got his sip of milk.

GIANTS IN THE EARTH

I BROKE OFF FROM the chase of Stahr on the 29th of October, exhausted from lack of sleep and disheartened from watching her and the undersize cub continue to take their licks raiding. Two days later, at the very end of the month, Fernie and her cubs were on a horse ranch of several hundred acres by the Swan River. They had arrived at that spot by following the series of scent drags laid down by the team. Hidden within a forested stretch, they were feeding on the latest in the sequence of meat piles offered them. The cache included the usual automobile-smooshed deer plus part of a moose found dead on the highway's shoulder. RKR was what the team christened their strategy—roadkill redistribution. The ranch owner was delighted to be of help, and the bear family had been sitting tight for several days.

Everything seemed to be going along as well as could be wished for, which, with grizzlies, is a good time to grit your teeth and start looking around to see what sort of trouble you missed. That afternoon, the bear team lost Fernie's radio signal. They scrambled across the general area with their receivers tweaked to high volume, but all anyone came up with was a faint, untrustworthy transmission from somewhere toward the Swan Mountains.

Two days later, on November 2, Tim Manley's colleague Erik Wenum took an airplane flight to pin down the locations of a number of bears. Wenum tends to handle black bears (along with mountain lions, moose, and deer) for this district of the Montana Fish, Wildlife & Parks Department, while Manley specializes in grizz.

But because both men have so much corrugated country to cover, and neither can ever be sure which type of bear he'll find in a yard or a culvert trap, they routinely fill in for each other. When Wenum reached a good altitude in the aircraft, he switched over to Fernie's frequency to see what he could pick up, if anything. He got her. She was near Crevice Lake atop the Swan Range.

Counting the various caches put out to gradually lure Fernie and the cubs eastward, the family had consumed upwards of a thousand pounds of game meat. Plus 300 pounds of apples gathered by the bear team and donated by people in the area. Given the bears' location amid the snowy summits, they were almost certainly preparing to hibernate. They would be going into their underground chamber fat and sassy. Manley flew about a week later and confirmed that the family had denned near another lake on a slope just above tree line.

When Manley telephoned and started bringing me up-to-date, I kept waiting for the catch, the caveat. There wasn't one. The impromptu plan had worked, period. Nobody got hurt. No citizens suffered serious property damage or the loss of more than a few dollars' worth of bird seed or grain. Fernie and her offspring were alive and well with the energy reserves to endure the worst a Montana winter could throw at them. Congratulations were due all around.

— — —

Hunt's contract ended after October. On a quiet day before she left for her home on the east side of Utah's Wasatch Mountains, she told me she had known by the age of eight that she wanted to work with big carnivores. Her career started at Sea World, where she was one of their first female marine mammal trainers. She proceeded to the University of Montana and teamed up with Charles Jonkel, a lifelong bear researcher and for several years the leader of collaborative grizzly bear studies in northern Montana. Beginning in 1982, Jonkel and Hunt undertook a series of experiments to test chemical repellents on captive bears. Hunt then helped promote use of the repellent found to be most effective—capsicum spray, derived from red chili peppers.

If you've ever handled spicy chili powder and accidentally rubbed some in your eyes or nose, you already know the feeling of having those organs set on fire by the active ingredient, capsaicin. And you can appreciate how a dose of this superirritant might affect an animal whose nasal passages make up the better part of its face and house one of the most exquisite senses of smell among mammals. First developed commercially by a Montanan, Bill Pounds, pepper spray is now widely sold in a canister with a thumb-levered plunger on top. Capsicum suffused in a heavy oil base shoots out for twenty feet or more, forming an orange-pink, noxious, thoroughly discombobulating mist.

State and federal officials were at first leery of what looked like a gimmick—a quick fix, too good to be true. (Just spray those pesky bruins away with new, improved ____!) Today, they urge recreationists and hunters alike to take canisters along, ready for instant use. Much as pepper spray has become standard equipment in big-city law enforcement, largely replacing mace, it is becoming hard to find a backpacker in grizzly country like Glacier, Yellowstone, or Banff National Park who doesn't carry a canister in a quick-draw holster attached to a belt or pack strap.

Canada won't allow pistols in the country, and you can't carry firearms in U.S. national parks. Even where you can tote a gun, there are a hundred ways for things to go from bad to worse trying to hit and kill a grizzly with bullets. By contrast, you can hardly miss with pepper spray, no matter how frantically your hands might be shaking. After conducting a review of close encounters with grizzlies believed to be acting aggressively, Stephen Herrero, a bear behavior expert based in Alberta, found the pepper spray to be effective 94 percent of the time it was used.

In addition to saving dozens of people from a possible mauling, this relatively low-tech invention has also kept in good health any number of grizzlies that would otherwise have been wounded or killed by people firing bullets into animals merely rearing up for a better look, approaching out of curiosity, or, at worst, making a conventional bluff charge.

Having relied on noxious aerosol spray for millennia, skunks benefit from the fact that it not only deters attacks but teaches future avoidance. In other words, it is a highly effective aversive conditioning technique in its own right. The Montana grizzly teachers and other bear conflict specialists sometimes use pepper spray to greet a visiting bear on the threshold of a food storage area. But it's a passive setup; the canisters are anchored in place and rigged to trip wires. A manager practicing active deterrence obviously needs to be able to operate from a greater distance.

The first systematic field trials of any kind related to aversive conditioning for grizzlies took place during the late 1970s under the guidance of John Dolly-Molly, a bear specialist in Denali National Park, Alaska. His team tried using rubber dumdums to sting bears. That simple advance gave them a handle on grizz that persisted in approaching visitors or their campsites too closely, a seemingly intractable problem in the northern half of the huge reserve, where the tundra offers no tree tall enough to hang food in, much less climb. During my first visit to Denali, in the early 1980s, I met a ranger-biologist named Joe Van Horn as he was setting up a dummy tent in the vicinity of a known troublemaker. Rather than wait for the bear to make its next move on a real camp, he explained, the plan was to lure the animal in and make it wish it wouldn't find another tent for a long time. In other words, grizzly education had already gone proactive.

Several years later, Yellowstone Park and the Wyoming Game and Fish Department decided to include aversive conditioning as part of the grizzly management program for the Greater Yellowstone Ecosystem. Hunt was called in to put problem bears there through deterrence sessions with dumdum rounds. But these projectiles are effective only to about forty yards. It wasn't long before Hunt felt the need for something in the arsenal that could reach out still farther and in more dramatic fashion to leave a longer-lasting impression. After hearing about the breed of dogs trained to chase and hold bears in the Old World, she acquired her first Karelian in 1992.

In a general sense, you could trace bear education at least as far back as settlers who blasted nosy ones with shotgun loads of rock salt. Without a great deal more effort, you could probably make the case that aversive conditioning is as ancient as the relationship between *Homo sapiens* and *Canis familiaris.* Camp-follower canines—or however you might characterize animals in transition between wolves and dogs—surely served not only to alert human bands but also to distract and deter potential marauders.

The more dogs a modern-day cattle or sheep operation keeps around, the fewer the bear problems. Having often heard this firsthand from stockmen, Hunt originally envisioned putting Karelians to work as guard dogs on ranches where depredations by grizzlies were a recurring problem and a continual cause of bear deaths. Then she got the Karelian named Cassie. Hunt was struck by the animal's intensity when pursuing a target and by her responsiveness to people, two traits that don't always emerge together in hunting dogs. The more closely Hunt watched her new companion, the wider the possibilities seemed.

Hunt bred Cassie to the male called Rio. Around that time, she was hired for a straightforward study of black bear biology in New Mexico by the Hornocker Wildlife Research Institute. As a sort of sideline, she began trying out the dogs when people called to report bear incidents. Encouraged by the results, she assembled a pack including Cassie, Rio, and their offspring and set off with them for the prime proving grounds of Yosemite National Park. The place is well populated by black bears and perpetually stuffed with visitors during the nonwinter months. If only one in 100 is heedless with food, that still amounts to thousands weekly giving the reserve's bears an opportunity to learn that the fat of the land is most easily found inside cars and campgrounds these days. In addition to the danger that these smash-and-grab bruins present, they cause hundreds of thousands of dollars' worth of damage annually to automobiles alone.

While traveling through Yosemite during 1996 to hike and take in the sights, I happened to find myself about an hour or two behind Hunt at several stops. I'd heard of her work but had never met her. My curiosity mounted by the day. Visitors at every trailhead and campground seemed to be talking about "the woman with the bear dogs." The sight of busted car windows and tourists huddled off to the side while some bear bounced on a picnic table trying to open a food cooler made it easy to guess why. At the same time, I could understand why Hunt never seemed to stay in one place long enough for me to catch up. She plainly needed to be everywhere at once.

After Yosemite, Hunt and her canine SWAT team did brief stints in other areas, including Glacier Park, handling both black and grizzly bears. She then began contracting with the Montana Department of Fish, Wildlife & Parks to try to help them get a handle on problem grizzlies and the consequent legal and illegal killing of the bears, which had escalated over the years to levels that threatened to derail the recovery effort.

The years required for a grizzly to grow to maturity and begin reproducing meant that many of the Flathead area bears Hunt worked with had long careers ahead of them—if they kept their weakness for artificial food in check. Having come to feel personally responsible for those animals to some extent, she wanted to return and keep providing encouragement as long as funding stayed available for the program.

— — —

In early November, Stahr and her surviving cub disappeared in the brush near Hay Creek, not far off the North Fork road and about half a mile from my property. Her signal stayed unusually stationary, which was cause for concern. Manley could all too easily envision her dead or wounded, shot or possibly creamed by an automobile. The most hopeful alternative was that she was on the carcass of some other animal struck by a car or a hunter's bullet. Working without Hunt or her dogs now that the Wind River Bear Institute's contract for that year had ended, he put off bushwhacking in to see what was going on. His own safety aside, he didn't want to risk disturbing the bear. If Stahr had simply settled down for a while, that was the best thing she could be doing.

Over the next few days, reports started trickling in from logging truck drivers and other travelers who were seeing a cub crossing the road or wandering alongside it near Hay Creek. They said that the little grizzly was always alone. For a grizzly cub of the year to go more than a short sprint away from its mother is such a rare occurrence that it underscored Manley's fear that Stahr was a goner.

But no, Stahr was indeed on a road-killed deer, and Manley saw her again on November 5. He did not, however, see the cub. The following day, Stahr was back at Home Ranch Bottom, following the old trail of an elk carcass dragged through a pasture by a successful hunter. Once again, she was alone. The cub was nowhere to be found north or south. It must have left in desperation or been kicked out by its mother. If there were some other explanation, some warmer, more satisfying vignette to be told, nobody knew what that might be.

Did Stahr perhaps recognize that her cub was not going to outlast the coming winter? Was it already ill and faltering? Somehow, hogging food for herself and driving off the youngster didn't seem to fit with the tendency of grizzly mothers to unhesitatingly defend their young from perceived threats by much larger males or wolf packs—or humans. It may be that we just do not know very much about the behavior of grizzlies under severe nutritional stress. Or it may be that Stahr was behaving atypically even for a very hungry mother, as if we needed another reminder that no two grizzlies are quite alike. What else was there to say?

She hung around Home Ranch Bottom a while, then moved south to the property of a neighbor I'll call Jake. With the opening weeks of hunting season winding down and fewer orange-clad troops stalking hither and yon, Manley finally made the decision to feed Stahr as he had Fernie. Jake owned a good chunk of ground, and Manley asked him to allow Stahr to stay in his acreage and dine on a donated deer.

Jake considered the proposition. He weighed in the fact that he himself liked to feed wildlife in the winter, though to him that meant feeding the deer. He also thought about the elk he had recently killed and now had hanging in his garage to season. Manley reminded him that Stahr already knew it was there and would surely be back to learn more about its availability. Okay, said Jake, and he helped Manley drag a road-killed deer from the house site to a thickly forested part of his property, laying down a scent trail for Stahr to follow.

The grizzly stayed on the deer meat for five days, after which she returned to Home Ranch Bottom. By now, it was mid-November. Stahr found enough to keep her interested in the ranch area for the next few days and then began traveling from there to a dozen other homesites in the valley. "She's just taking us to everybody's place where she got stuff before," Manley observed. "To us, it's a big problem. But going and finding food in places they remember, places where they know they are likely to find more—that's what grizzlies are supposed to do."

Toward the final week of November, the riverside aspens and cottonwoods stood bare. Snow coated the leaves fallen at their feet. In the high country, the powder was deep and piling up taller by the day. Stahr abruptly changed her pattern and walked south to the confluence of the North Fork and Middle Fork and into a rural area called Blankenship. On the 25th, she was on Smokey Bear Lane dragging a deer carcass out of a guy's shed along with the heads of other deer killed by his buddies during hunting season. Manley set out a culvert trap but couldn't catch her. Since she wouldn't go inside the big, steel cylinder, he did. Using it as a protective blind—the shark cage approach—he waited with his dart gun for the grizzly to come in. In the end, one of the snares he had hidden by the bait did the job instead, gripping Stahr unyieldingly by a well-traveled paw.

— — —

By November's end, most young bears and adult females have been asleep for a while, and most adult males are either denned up as well or very close to it. The exceptions in the Flathead are a few big, burly, and therefore cold-resistant males still out making a good living off hunters' leavings—gut piles and the carcasses of animals fatally wounded but never tracked down.

During the late 1980s and 1990s, a series of easy winters led to some of the highest numbers of deer and elk anyone could remember in the North Fork. The colonizing wolf population expanded. Cougar numbers climbed. Researchers began to notice the odd male grizzly staying out much of the winter scavenging the leftovers from successful hunts by the wolves and big cats.

In presettlement times of wildlife abundance, that sort of activity may have been much more common. It seems to be a matter of energy intake versus energy output. As long as the balance stays favorable, a grizzly has no pressing need to dig into a hillside and snooze the cold months away. Black bears become truly dormant over winter with lowered rates of heartbeat and respiration. In *Ursus arctos horribilis,* the basal metabolic rate slows by one-quarter to one-third when the animal is asleep in its den, but this is more like a nap from which a grizz can awaken anytime. In the comparatively mild climate of coastal areas such as Kodiak Island, biologists occasionally find grizzlies out and about every month of the year. Some will excavate a den but then retire to it only for short periods, or else simply lie around outside the entrance, taking things easy. To come upon fresh tracks in the Rockies during a January warm spell has never been uncommon, and there is one record of a grizzly chasing down elk in Yellowstone during a midwinter thaw.

For all that, ever shorter days and deeper snows generally bring about a clear end to grizzly bear activity in the mountains. So when Chris Servheen, the grizzly bear recovery coordinator for the U.S. Fish & Wildlife Service, gave an interview to the western Montana newspaper *The Missoulian* on November 29, 1998, it was intended as a kind of summing up for the year.

Servheen began his state-of-the-grizz report with an update on the Greater Yellowstone Ecosystem. The 400 to 600 grizzlies currently estimated for that 9,500-square-mile area amounted to twice as many grizzlies as it had harbored in 1975, when the great bear was listed as threatened south of Canada and efforts to restore the species began. Similarly, whereas almost no grizzlies were known from the 1,200-square-mile Selkirk Ecosystem of northern Idaho in 1975, the area held two to three dozen at the time that Servheen made his report.

No more than a handful could be found in the 10,000-square-mile North Cascades Ecosystem in northern Washington, if that many. The situation for the 2,600-square-mile Cabinet-Yaak Ecosystem in western Montana was grim enough that the steadily dwindling population (of perhaps no more than a score of grizz) should probably be listed as endangered rather than threatened, Servheen said. But as in the Selkirks and the southern reaches of the Greater Yellowstone Ecosystem, the 9,600-square-mile Northern Continental Divide Ecosystem, or NCDE, had grizzlies showing up in all sorts of places where none used to be seen. A prime example was the Rocky Mountain Front, east of the continental divide. Grizz there had gone from a memory in 1975 to a fact of daily life. The big worry in the NCDE remained deaths from human causes. Indeed, that was still the big worry everywhere.

About 90 percent of the grizzly deaths that authorities find out about are caused by humans. Half of all the known grizzly bear mortality in the contiguous states since 1983 has taken place on private lands, and nearly two-thirds of the grizzly bear mortalities in the NCDE occurred on or near private holdings. Yet private lands make up only 2 percent of the Greater Yellowstone Ecosystem and 16 percent of the NCDE. (Meeting with Servheen personally at various times, I noticed that he used the term *private lands* more or less interchangeably with "time bombs for grizzlies" and "land mines for bears.") Servheen concluded by saying that he was troubled by the number of human-caused deaths in the NCDE during 1998. The total was twenty-two, the highest in years.

About the time the newspaper was being printed and Manley snared Stahr, the total moved up to twenty-three. Someone shot Louie. It happened near the subdivision with the clover-seeded yard where I had first met him. I'd wondered if a grizzly that blasé about being exposed to view would make it through the hunting season with so many gunners abroad. Now I knew. At a mere 200 pounds, the three-year-old should have been in a den that day. But the lack of berries through the late summer and fall had kept poorly nourished grizz of all ages roaming way beyond their normal bedtime. Louie had been one of them. Stahr was another.

— — —

On the first day of December, Manley released Stahr in the northwest corner of Glacier Park, thinking that, with the road-killed deer she had found, the one he donated, and sundry pilfered tidbits, she might be ready to den. No luck. The next day, she was on the west side of the North Fork eating a trapper's collection of recently skinned marten skulls. The day after that, she was fifteen miles downstream at Home Ranch Bottom. Two days later, she was another twenty miles downstream at Blankenship, visiting the house at which she had just been captured.

Manley had to go to the north end of the U.S. part of the North Fork and deal with No. 47, the twenty-nine-year-old male first captured for research in Canada. The big animal had tried breaking into occupied structures, which meant that his fate was sealed. He was caught and euthanized, bringing the total of human-caused deaths in the NCDE to twenty-four. Stahr seemed determined to add to what was already a recent record and make the total twenty-five. She went south of Blankenship to a resort spot called Lake Five, then to a KOA campground by U.S. Highway 2, before returning to the garage where she had found the deer heads.

Manley was still firing cracker shells at her, keeping her somewhat at bay as she stormed her way on into the middle of December. She was quite possibly the last female grizzly out roaming that year. Manley would rather have been thinking about Christmas shopping or skiing or anything but rogue grizzlies by then. Frustrated, he fed her again, placing another roadkill out in a safe spot by Blankenship. That was on the 15th. On the 17th, Stahr was thirty miles north and a couple thousand feet higher in altitude, by Longbow Lake. The snow was too deep for her to reach her old denning area. She dug her way into the mountainside lower down by the base of a waterfall and at last went to sleep.

INTERLUDE:

REAL BEAR CLAWING THE BACKBONE OF THE WORLD

I GO GRIZZLY WATCHING most every autumn in the portion of Glacier National Park that lies east of the Continental Divide. The country is drier and more open than the Flathead watershed on the heavily forested west side, and bears are far easier to keep in view. My hikes follow a series of high, windy valleys roughed into broad troughs by past glaciation, sided with thick bands of uplifted sediments from the bottom of Precambrian seas, and capped by more sharply honed tiers that aspire to ultraviolet reaches of the sky. There is almost a full mile of vertical relief between the valley floors and the crags, and you wouldn't want to change a single feature in between. In a 1998 movie about the afterlife, I noticed some of these settings used as the backdrop for Heaven. They are surely as lovely as any place you could ever walk here on Earth.

With workable weather, constant scanning through binoculars, and some luck, I might locate as many as a dozen grizz during a day's east side hike. In the fall of 1998, the year of widespread berry crop failure, I spied bears all over the mountainsides. But they were the other kind—black bears. Adept tree climbers, black bears normally keep to forested habitats where they have a better chance of escaping enemies. Grizz, known to dine on their smaller cousins, are high on the list of threats. That made it all the more intriguing to find black bears foraging for hours on end across the open slopes where grizzlies should have been.

I'd heard a lot of reports about east side grizzlies patrolling for food at lower elevations that year, much as on the west side. Dan Carney, the bear management specialist for the Blackfeet Fish & Wildlife Department, confirmed the pattern. Most of the radio-collared grizz he kept track of had left the protected wildlands of the high country for the Blackfeet reservation and were wandering the foothills and the edge of the Great Plains. I took the daily presence of black bears on grizzly turf in Glacier as equally strong proof that the silvertips widely considered to be park bears were somewhere else.

To distinguish grizzlies from black bears, the Blackfeet spoke of the larger species as Real Bear. That's how I thought of grizz on the east side too, especially that year. These were no more park bears than they were Blackfeet bears, national forest bears, backyard bears—everybody's bears and nobody's bears. They were real bears, doing whatever they had to, wherever they needed to be, in the real world of 1998.

During the first of my trips to Glacier's east side another year—a decent one for wild fruits—I found grizzlies in their usual September haunts on the valleys' floors and lower slopes, mouths stained purple from rummaging through huckleberry and serviceberry branches. Now and then, they added buffaloberries, chokecherries, wild currants, and mountain ash berries to the mix. I returned in mid-October after most of the berries were gone. Instead of trekking all over as I usually did, I spent a week watching a solitary grizzly work its way around the side of a mountain and up toward its crown.

The bear was a large, dark brown, well-fed adult with a luxuriant coat grown out in anticipation of winter. Not for another year would its fur appear so shiny and new, much less cover a midsection so round or a rump so wide, rippling with stored fat. This was a prosperous-looking bruin, portly, baronial—one big-ass bale of life force. I want to tell the tale of our meeting on top of the world.

Winter had already claimed the highest elevations. Coated with fresh crystals, the strata above 8,000 feet gleamed like bands of pure marble or chalk. The slopes below were just on the cusp, with the east side gusts sometimes slinging rain, sometimes sleet, and occasionally blizzards. Then the sun would break through to soften the snowflakes and send meltwater trickling over the cliff ledges. An hour later, the rivulets might be frozen and the ledges glassy with newborn ice while another tempest brewed.

In the beginning, the grizzly was on a south-facing talus slope toward the base of the mountain. Bighorn sheep grazed to one side. Mountain goats lay bedded among broken cliffs on the other. Preoccupied with digging for roots, the bear paid no attention as I climbed within viewing range—not close, just near enough to pick out details with a fifteen- to forty-five-power telescope. On a later day, the grizzly was going after more roots by scraping away the thin topsoil on ledges, when a herd of bighorn ewes and young crossed above. They bedded down less than 200 feet away. One ewe walked downhill to within 100 feet for a closer inspection. Though I've seen grizz chase bighorns in the Rockies and Dall's sheep in Alaska, the bear paid no more attention to that particular observer than to me hundreds of yards away.

A couple of days after that, the bear was halfway up the west-facing side of the mountain. I passed a moose in a brush-fringed meadow and a coyote nipping off old mountain ash berries before busting my way uphill through jungles of alder and false huckleberry, or snowbrush. I hit a maze of elk trails with fresh droppings and finally followed them out of the shrub tangles onto open talus. Above, purplish red layers of the silty limestone called argillite outcropped here and there in narrow belts. Their ledges held ground-hugging juniper shrubs and scattered copses of subalpine fir scores of years old but seldom more than head high.

Terrific winds were tumbling off the Great Divide. This was the first slope they hit. Braced against them, I made for a thicket of the stunted firs and scrunched down among the tough, springy branches.

Their bittersweet, turpentine scent enveloped me even in the gale. Each time the bear came within a few hundred yards, I began edging away toward another cluster of fir. More often than not, the animal would turn before I had to move, and my telescope would offer a rear-end view of featureless, wind-rippled fur. Only the longer hairs on the hump stood out, parting and fanning as the bear put its shoulder muscles to work.

The grizzly kept digging nonstop, unearthing roots of vetch, in the pea family, and lomatium, or biscuitroot, in the carrot family. It had been doing the same for days, raking through the talus whenever I first spotted it in the morning and when I last looked before leaving in late afternoon. Being in full hyperphagia, the prehibernation drive to put on as much fat as possible, the animal probably kept at it through much of the night. Virtually every step I took landed on part of a small crater, either freshly excavated or left from an earlier year and beginning to fill in with scree.

Scalloped by grizzly claws and dotted with grizzly droppings, much of the upper mountainside was loose and slidey, still seeking its angle of repose. The big sky was more than unsettled; it was hyper, reminding me of speeded-up movie scenes in which storms seem to gather and fade within moments. Migrating golden eagles shot through unraveling clouds, while swaths of sunlight and shadow raced one other across faraway slopes turned burgundy and gold. All this motion was framed by massive vaults of stone more than a billion years old, standing unperturbed, anchored in geologic time. Here was the realm the Blackfeet knew as the Backbone of the World.

The morning dawned bright when I began bushwhacking uphill with some companions on a different day, toward the end of the week. By the time I emerged from the snowbrush, clouds were piling up against the west side of the divide. They darkened and swelled at an impressive rate, chafing against the highest peaks. Yet the forward edge of the storm stayed brilliantly lit by strong sunlight from the east. Inner whorls flickered and glowed. A shimmering nimbus spread around the edges, and luminous streaks of vapor flared outward from that into the blue. If trumpeting archangels had paraded from this gloriole, you would have nodded and said, "Of course." Not to overdo the analogy, but as you ascend toward the upper limit of the life zone, you can't escape some of the feeling of having cast off earthly things to stand unadorned before powers far greater than your own. Add a grizzly, and the notion is entirely justified.

Real Bear, as I had come to think of this particular grizz, was higher and farther toward the head of the valley than on any day before. While I huffed that direction, the storm slipped its mountaintop moorings and began to surge east. The nearer you draw to the base of rock outcrops, the more thoroughly they screen the landscape above. I was thinking that Real Bear was still a considerable distance away and more to the north, when the animal abruptly appeared at the outer edge of a ledge looking straight downhill at me through a stinging rain.

It was a fixed stare, and grizzlies have better vision than many credit them with. Even so, I couldn't be sure whether Real Bear truly had me in view or was orienting partly by smell. I didn't think I was anywhere near close enough to be considered a threat, so I stopped and waited. Real Bear leaned forward, sifting the wind with flared nostrils, then sat on its rump and slowly waved its massive head back and forth.

Through binoculars, I looked for any sign of agitation or alarm. But the ears weren't laid back, the muzzle stayed smooth, the eyes soft. Real Bear seemed concerned only with testing the air more thoroughly. I wasn't too worried that catching my scent at that distance would spur the grizzly to react strongly one way or the other. Busy park trails intersected the berry patches and other prime habitats that the bears frequented on lower slopes earlier in the year, and most of the grizz hereabouts were somewhat conditioned to the scents and sounds of humans as a result. Every year or two, newspapers trumpet the news: Hiker Mauled in Glacier Park. Never once will they headline the truly astounding annual event that I would rather see publicized: 100,000-Plus Hikers with Varying

Levels of Skill and Intelligence Bumble through Glacier's Grizzly Country Unscathed.

Real Bear lay down facing my direction with its chin atop crossed paws. I dropped away downhill and moved farther toward the head of the valley. My plan was to negotiate a separate, taller section of the cliff belt. But the climb began to turn more and more iffy, and I couldn't be sure of where I would top out in relation to the grizzly if it moved. So I retraced my steps, making a wide swing down the valley to get around the ledge where Real Bear had been, until I could see the animal again. From there, I proceeded to scramble up another third of the mountainside. Perched nearly a quarter of a mile above, I could keep track of the bear now without it disappearing behind breaks among the cliffs or into the swales and runoff channels creasing the talus fields.

At the time, I considered my position to be comfortable from the standpoint of safety and poor only in terms of shelter. There was none. I was surrounded by sparse, low vegetation, rock debris, and grizzly-dug craters. The weather, already nasty, was deteriorating. With a foot in one pawed pit, I kicked with my other boot at the rubble heaped around it, trying to fashion a level shelf on which to stand. The wind kept flinging sleet sideways into my face. My boots were proving to have too many miles worn through the layers that were supposed to keep them water-resistant. I was damp and cold, and the gale made my eyes water, blurring my vision. Then it started to snow. And then I wasn't comfortable from the standpoint of safety either, because the bear had been slowly, barely noticeably, yet steadily, zigzagging uphill toward my spot.

The white squalls came in waves with stripes of sun dazzle between them, washing over thousands of vertical feet of rock walls in the background, over turquoise lakes pooled at their feet, over blackish green forests lining the valley floors, and across the long, open slope I was on. Real Bear was a sharply outlined figure with bright cinnamon and silver highlights one moment, a shadowy mass in a blur of snowflakes the next. A mass still moving uphill. During the peak of a squall, I crept higher on the talus. The grizzly went back and forth and even turned downslope for a short distance. Then it continued in my direction.

The allure of grizz and stories about them has always been bound up with the feeling of matching skills or wits with a potentially lethal beast. Even if the animal has other concerns and you only imagine that a matchup is happening, you face questions about the stuff you're made of. The person you liked to think you were just moments before, the things you held dear all those earlier days, the wisdom of your long-term goals—these are subjects suddenly up for review. And you may discover that what you want out of life above anything else, and what you would settle for, and what you never quite appreciated for the gift that it is, is to remain alive. Anything more counts as accessorizing.

What Real Bear would have made of my thoughts or what its intentions were, I couldn't say. The grizzly seemed careful to avoid looking directly my way as it neared. It was not terrifyingly close, and it was still absorbed in digging. On the other hand, I was three-quarters of the way up that mountain, so exposed on the slope and so far from escape cover that I was out of options and simply stood there tingling from my scalp to my marrow as though I had just seen the stars at midday. It was up to Real Bear now.

Water trickled off icicles on the sides of boulders. More water flowed under the ice encasing flat rocks, and the air bubbles squeezing between the stone and the crystal panes made wobbly abstractions. I remember gazing at them completely entranced. It could have been a trick of the mind to give itself a break. Or maybe my circuitry temporarily jammed. A beam of sunshine swept across a distant limestone palisade like a searchlight. The grizzly glanced at me out of the corner of its eye but kept its head down, feeding.

To warm my toes, I shifted from foot to foot, but smoothly so as not to make any attention-getting lurch. I listened to the sound of blood pulsing in my ears. Dried sulfurflower stalks shivered in the wind and loosed the snow gathered on their small umbels. Real Bear shook the moisture off its coat and glanced at me again. When it turned to feed along a different tangent, quartering away, I walked slowly in the other direction, stepping from crater to crater, one eye on my footing, the other on the grizzly.

Real Bear kept digging. Speeding up my pace, I went farther to the side and started angling downslope. I dropped over a ledge and landed on a fresh set of excavations—deep ones, probably to unearth ground squirrels, judging from the intact burrows around. I kept going. When, at last, I paused for a long look back, Real Bear merely had its nose down in a new pit.

My thoughts had progressed from "Please, bear" to "Thank you, bear" to "Damn, this must be the hardest-working grizz in the getting-fat business." And it could scarcely be going about its labors farther from people, their homes, or any kind of trouble, I reminded myself. The problem animal here, the one pushing the boundaries of acceptable behavior, has two legs. My legs. The bear, and only the bear, conducted itself honorably the whole time.

An hour later, I finally hit the forest toward the valley bottom and walked out of the drainage, and that was it for grizz-watching in the tall country that year. The next year, I went back and found Real Bear, or its twin. Same size, same color, same place, digging away. As before, I was hard put to find a section of the slope that hadn't been altered by grizzly toil. Real Bear was single-pawedly tearing the face off a mountain.

Given the sheer numbers of hoary marmots, golden-mantled ground squirrels, Columbian ground squirrels, pocket mice, and voles in the high country, you would expect these ubiquitous burrowers to be the primary earth movers there. Yet according to a recent study in Glacier Park, silvertips shift more soil than any other wildlife in the alpine and subalpine zones. One of the reasons grizzlies turn over so much ground is to get at all the aforementioned rodents, especially those hibernating when the bears are not. For the most part, though, the big omnivores are hunting the nutrients stored in plant roots and bulbs.

Grizz scarify and disturb countless acres this way in the short run. Over time, they end up fashioning richer, more varied plant communities. Raking and plowing swaths across a landscape, the bears loose countless seeds and spread them around. They also plant them in improved soil, because all that excavating brings scarce nitrogen from lower ground levels to the surface, the result farmers seek when they till their fields. This fertilizing effect causes vegetation such as glacier lilies and spring beauties to grow more vigorously and produce more seeds than they do in undisturbed sites. Though it is hardly part of their public persona, grizzlies are, in effect, big-time wildflower gardeners.

You'll find similar grizzly-modified habitats down low on riverbanks and gravel bars, where the search for the starchy roots of a vetch called *Hedysarum* leaves the ground contoured like a practice range for small mortars. In Alaska, I found stretches of Brooks Range tundra reworked by grizz into that same oversize egg carton pattern for miles along well-drained hillsides and old moraines. Dan Carney showed me where grizzlies had been digging in rangelands out on the high plains, mainly for roots but also to get into the brood chambers of hornets that nest underground.

Nearly every grizzly that Carney radio-tags and follows dens high on Glacier's snow-buried mountainsides. Upon awakening months later, a large percentage exits the park for the early green-up lower down. Keeping close to woodland groves and streamside brush for cover when near human territory, some stay on while spring gives way to summer. Others move back into the park as soon as the melt starts up the big valleys.

Around midsummer, a number of grizzlies continue upward all the way to the peaks. They are after army cutworm moths, which migrate from the prairies to spend the warm months close to the very crest of the Continental Divide. The insects sip nectar from alpine flower fields (partly cultivated by grizz) through the night, pollinating blossoms as they go. By day, they shelter beneath rock rubble, congregating on certain talus slopes or boulder fields in astronomical numbers. The moths stay until early fall, and a good many grizzlies stick with them, overturning stones to lick up the diminutive prey.

When the moths first arrive in the high country, their bodies are about 40 percent fat. By fall, they have abdomens plump as jelly beans from weeks of lapping plant sugars and are closer to three-quarters fat. That makes them the richest source of energy a grizzly can tap in the ecosystem. Pound for pound, these winged nougats provide more calories than roots, berries, nuts, or, for that matter, straight red meat.

Although biologists have counted as many as two dozen grizzlies feeding together on moths in a single talus field, the number of such insect lodes is limited. Once berries begin to ripen in mid-August, fruit becomes the most widespread and abundant of all bear meals in this stretch of the Rockies. By late September, that bounty is fading, the moths are leaving to overwinter on the Great Plains, and some bears abandon the park again to forage down in the foothills and beyond, only to turn around with the coming of winter and journey to the reserve's lofty slopes to sleep.

In light of all the back-and-forth movement, this population never really qualified as park bears. There were individuals that spent a great deal of time inside the protected part of the ecosystem, and individuals that spent less. Before grizzlies were safeguarded under the Endangered Species Act, those that went beyond the sanctuary simply kept getting picked off. The deaths were not always reported; bears just disappeared. If you went to count grizz, you found so few outside the reserve that it looked as though the bears strongly favored parklands. Thus, when officials first sketched out what they considered to be habitat essential to grizzly recovery, they drew the eastern limit right along Glacier's eastern boundary.

Carney told me, "After a few years, we looked over our locations for radioed bears and realized we'd better move the line about ten miles farther east to Highway 464. Now I've got bears roaming way east of there. One nearly made it to Cutbank [a town about forty miles outside of the park]."

Whether you're among east side cowboys, west side loggers, or Montanans in general, if the discussion turns to bears and efforts to save them, it seems that someone sooner or later asks: What good is a grizzly anyway? When I visit an animal like Real Bear along the Backbone of the World, the setting is so charged with wild beauty, the experience so strong and unalloyed, that it never fails to answer the question. Grizz strengthen the spirit. They create wonder. They humble. They temper. They clarify and awaken. They do me a world of good.

I don't recall observing a grizzly that looked like Real Bear on the park's east side during the bad berry year of 1998. Haphazard as my surveys are, the animal could easily have been around. I probably overlooked it or else didn't recognize it. Then again, it could well have been out on national forest, tribal, or private lands with the other grizz. It probably visited nonpark sites every year at some point before returning to the mountainside in Glacier where I observed it digging day after day.

So even as I am watching real bears walk close to the heavens, having myself a pure nature binge and romanticizing away, I try to keep in mind that the lives of these same animals depend from time to time upon what goes on in the less perfect, more worldly dimensions of the ecosystem. Grizz will recover only to the extent that we guarantee them some room there beside us.

SO, WHAT WOULD YOU HAVE DONE?

IN MARCH OF 1999, the local newspaper carried an article on Carrie Hunt and her Wind River Bear Institute crew, dogs included of course. The report described them as having worked on twenty-nine grizzlies and thirty-nine black bears during the difficult year of 1998. They were credited with directly helping to save fourteen of the grizz. Other articles appearing around that time warned of a rough spring ahead where bears were concerned. Many had gone into hibernation with less than a full fuel tank. As a result, some were already out in late March, about a month earlier than average. Among them was a starving black bear cub that made its way through the snow to a home and was found collapsed on the porch, too weak to lift its head.

For a number of grizz, it did prove to be a difficult spring. Here's what Stahr did to create problems after she emerged from her den in 1999: Nothing. As Carrie Hunt would say, Stahr was being a good bear. She spent most of her days on the Glacier Park side of the North Fork, passed the late summer and fall in huckleberry patches as good grizzly bears will, and denned during the usual period, the latter part of October, in the Longbow Lake area again.

Through the spring and early summer of that year, Fernie and her cubs, now yearlings, remained a success story as well. They stayed in the backcountry just being grizzly bears, wild and independent. Trouble-free. On the 17th of July, a twenty-year-old man camping alone at an alpine lake in the part of the Swans' crest known as Jewel Basin settled into a green creek bank at the lake's inlet to read a book. Hearing splashing, he looked up and saw a mother grizzly with two yearling cubs walking toward his tent, which was some distance away.

The man jumped up, ran to a tree, and tried to climb it. But the subalpine fir was so small he could barely get off the ground. He ran to a second tree and started to climb. It was also a runt. The guy could go no higher than six to eight feet. He probably looked ridiculous swaying atop that skinny, cold-stunted conifer. But I would bet that his appearance was the last thing he was worrying about; and as someone who once climbed a thickly limbed spruce to avoid a grizzly, only to realize twenty feet up that he was still wearing snowshoes, I am not qualified to comment on a man's choice of escape routes under duress.

This camper had packed along pepper spray. Unfortunately, the canister had fallen out of its holster and been lost sometime during his hike to Jewel Basin. He had also brought a pistol, and he had that with him in the tree. As the grizzlies proceeded closer to his tent, he began yelling and shooting into the air, intending to frighten them away. He got their full attention instead. The mother bear turned, headed in his direction, and began sniffing the base of a tree thirty feet from him. He yelled some more. She came toward the tree to which he was clinging. The bear didn't charge or show signs of aggression such as flattening her ears or popping her jaws, but she did walk straight over. At which point, the man shot and killed Fernie.

That was his story as told to Manley and others during a subsequent investigation. The fellow was keyed up about grizzly bears to begin with and understandably got somewhat panicky. Everyone agreed that he could have made better choices—like simply leaving—between the time he first spied the bear family and the moment he pulled the trigger. On the other hand, he could have been injured or killed by a grizzly bear, and he did what he could with that in mind. Fernie's career was over eight years after she was born.

In losing their mother, the juveniles lost their repository of home-range knowledge and their defense against bigger bears. Their reaction was to make their way back to the Ferndale area. There were few, if any, other grizzlies to contend with down in the valley in mid-summer of 1999, and it was where the young animals remembered finding the most food during their first year of life.

Toward the end of 1998, the team renamed the cubs, which they had been calling Nip and Tuck. The female became Claire, after the owner of the horse ranch who allowed them to feed the bears there, and the male was called Speedo to honor his early Hungry Horse Reservoir swimming accomplishments. Both carried microchips implanted just under their skin so they could be identified. At eighteen months of age, the orphans were still too small to be fitted with radio collars, which would be pulled off by the bears if put on loosely but would choke the animals as they grew if fixed more snugly around their necks. Manley needed to monitor their movements, nonetheless. He set out to free-range them—shoot them with a drug-bearing dart—and affix ear tags containing miniature transmitters.

Claire proved elusive, but Manley managed to dart Speedo. He translocated the male to the South Fork near Whitcomb Creek. The young bear was back in a week. By connecting intermediate radio locations, Manley concluded that Speedo had swum the reservoir again. In any case, the yearling male found his sister, and the pair began hanging around Swan Horseshoe, the area where they had been captured with Fernie in 1998 and to which they had returned to spend the latter part of that fall. On August 20, 1999, the team caught both juveniles again. They were moved about thirty-five miles to Puzzle Creek near Marias Pass on the Continental Divide, which set them up nicely between the pristine terrain of Glacier Park and the Great Bear Wilderness immediately to the south.

Within two weeks, the siblings were back in the lower Swan Valley. Both of them had crossed into the South Fork drainage and swum Hungry Horse Reservoir once more. Manley went to free-range them and this time got Claire. He moved her twice as far, roughly seventy miles, and across the divide to the Rocky Mountain

Front. She was released into the Blackleaf Wildlife Management Area, habitat owned by the state near the eastern edge of the Bob Marshall Wilderness. Speedo, caught in a culvert trap soon afterward, was taken to the same general locale.

A week after that, in mid-September, Speedo had crossed back over the divide and was making his way west down the Middle Fork of the Flathead. Manley got him in a culvert trap yet again. It's possible that Speedo wasn't the brightest grizzly to ever wander the Rockies' heart. But it is also true that, just as some grizz will never set foot near another trap after their first experience, a few don't seem to mind being trapped all that much, possibly having learned that it is a sure way to get food, or because they are irredeemably curious. There is no reason to expect bears' motives to be less varied than their backgrounds and personalities.

During that same summer of 1999, Rick Sinott, employed by the Alaska Department of Fish and Game, was chasing two newly independent, possibly orphaned grizzly siblings on a circuit through the suburbs of fast-growing Anchorage. "They seemed to be around elementary schools a lot," he told me as we traveled together on the trail of other city-edge bears, "maybe because the schoolyards still have tree cover. They didn't bother any kids. They were mostly terrorizing parents."

The young male of the pair developed a habit of visiting the Anchorage zoo, also on the outskirts of town. He would go to the cage of an 800-pound male there and play with it through the bars. Sinott watched the subadult racing back and forth around the big bear's cage. Every now and then, the young grizzly would stop and touch paws with the big male, and they would sniff one another. The smaller bear kept eluding Sinott and returning to the zoo until personnel there finally darted him. He was put in a cage. After a while, they transferred him to Duluth, Minnesota, to live on display, known forever more as the Grizzly That Broke into the Zoo.

Tim Manley hauled Speedo to the North Fork and released the young bear in a drainage with a good crop of berries. "That was the last we ever heard of him," Manley told me. "We never found his signal again. We couldn't mark him down as a known mortality, so, technically, he is still alive. But who knows? We sure don't."

Claire didn't try to come back west as her brother had. She went east. In fact, she headed well out from the Rocky Mountain Front onto the start of the Great Plains, as if bent on reestablishing grizzly bears in the old buffalo country. She wasn't the first to try in recent years. Called upon to snare-trap one prairie-bound grizz bothering a rancher east of Glacier Park, Dan Carney, the Blackfeet Tribe's bear specialist, told me, "I was so far out on the plains I couldn't find a tree anywhere to anchor the cable to."

Claire wound up breaking into beehives. Mike Madel, Manley's counterpart on the Front for the state wildlife department, free-ranged her in a windbreak among wide-open wheat fields. He called Manley and said, "You can have your bear back. I insist." So Manley took her up the North Fork and let her go not far from where he had turned Speedo loose. Claire went west over the Whitefish Range divide, got into bird feeders near Beaver Lake, then found a fresh cow carcass in a rancher's boneyard. As the rancher didn't want her around, Manley caught her on the 20th of November. Now that she had put on her second year's full growth, he gave her a radio collar and released her on the west side of the North Fork near Frozen Lake. She went right up the mountainside and denned on the north side of Tuchuck Peak, a roadless area proposed for wilderness status.

~ ~ ~

Soon it was January of 2000, the start of a fresh millennium. Across the North Fork valley from Claire, Stahr gave birth to two new cubs in her den among the high slopes of the Livingstone Range. She showed up with the babies in tow at a private residence in the North Fork the last week of May. This was a cabin where she had scored food in 1998. She visited another homesite she knew, and another, reverting to her outlaw ways. Maybe the extra demands of nursing two offspring pushed her over the edge. Hunt and Manley worked her through late May and June with the dogs and cracker shells when she came too close to houses or the main road. The result appeared to be a compromise. Stahr kept scouting out her favorite cabins but mostly those whose owners lived elsewhere part of the year or were temporarily gone. In between, she foraged on natural foods—or at least on clover. Seeded to help hold the soil on disturbed sites such as roadsides and new lawns, this non-native plant spreads into open habitats of its own accord. Clover is rich in nitrogen and draws both black and grizzly bears, which get nourishing meals in return for being visible in fairly accessible sites. It is not the best of trade-offs but is far from the worst.

While Stahr was going her willful way up the North Fork that June, I was in northern Idaho's Selkirk Mountains. The area, which is chiefly national forest acreage, harbors a residual population of between fifty and seventy to possibly eighty grizzlies. But since half of them occupy the Canadian end of the Selkirk Range at any given time, the United States can really only claim twenty-five to perhaps forty animals. Greg Johnson, an Idaho Department of Fish & Game conservation officer with a special interest in silvertips, was showing me where some had been probing new habitats on the mountains' margins and occasionally down into the Kootenai Valley to the east.

Predictably, those bears ran into problems. Which wasn't entirely bad news, as Johnson saw things. Like bears cruising east from the Front onto the Great Plains, where none had been seen for decades, such dispersal could reflect an increasing population. If so, grizz getting in trouble in new places wasn't so much a setback as a symptom of recovery. It was all in how you chose to look at it.

Considered basically defunct by the end of the 1960s, the Selkirk group had bounced back after the species was listed. Johnson believed the population continued to show a slight increase year by year. This was due to stricter law enforcement and better hunter education in tandem with the protection mandated by the Endangered Species Act. The single most effective change was the closure of logging roads during the spring black bear hunting season, when grizzlies had often been poached or killed by mistake, and again during the fall hunting season. It had taken a lawsuit to force the U.S. Forest Service to gate off those roads, but the federal agency had finally fulfilled its obligation to provide security for a threatened species, and the bears were responding. Similarly, many feel that closures within the vast webwork of national forest logging roads in the NCDE represent the single most important factor behind the apparent rebound of grizz there.

The small size of the Selkirk grizzly enclave remained a worry, though, as did its isolation. Replenishment from Canada was becoming less and less likely due to extensive new logging and road building in the British Columbia half of the Selkirks and in every direction beyond. The Selkirk bears were therefore vulnerable to inbreeding as well as to the sort of random catastrophe—severe drought, wildfire, epidemics of disease or parasites, and so on—that can sweep a little pocket of survivors on into oblivion.

What was needed, Johnson said, was movement between the north Idaho grizz and the next closest group, found in Montana's Cabinet-Yaak Ecosystem, which lies only about twenty miles east but is cut off from the Selkirks by the wide-open farmland of the Kootenai Valley. Since the Cabinet-Yaak population was as small as or smaller than that of the Selkirks and dwindling at a disheartening rate, it would be even better if the north Idaho bears were ultimately connected with the real stronghold, the Northern Continental Divide Ecosystem encompassing Glacier Park.

The link came about three days after Johnson told me that. A young female reported in the lowlands near Bonner's Ferry, Idaho, had an ear marker showing that she came from the NCDE. It was Claire. Her radio collar had ceased working over winter. No one knew where she had gone after emerging from her den that spring. Well, here she was, nearly ninety miles due west. For a grizzly as mobile as this two-year-old female had been the previous year, that wasn't a huge distance, but it was enough.

In terms of potentially improving gene flow for the species,

Claire was doing splendidly. As for meeting other standards of hoped-for behavior, she wasn't doing too well. To be specific, she was getting into bird feeders in the valley. As Manley later said with a head shake of resignation, "They were bird seed bears, she and her brother both." Raised on the stuff, they couldn't seem to keep away. Maybe they thought they were supposed to seek it out. Perhaps not, but the temptation was so prevalent they couldn't stay clean. Claire was arrested.

Biologists had discussed the possibility of hauling in grizzlies to supplement small, outlier populations such as that in the Selkirks. They had even started transplanting silvertips into the Cabinet-Yaak before the program was cut, partly as a result of political pressure from logging interests. Yet current protocols would have made it very difficult to allow a known problem grizzly such as Claire to be released into either ecosystem. Managers were also reluctant to transplant her there, because that would have meant having to count her as another female subtracted from the NCDE. The decision was made to bring her home. Manley strapped a new radio collar on the bear and tucked her up into the North Fork watershed once more, about five miles south of the Canadian line.

She moved from the valley's west side into Glacier Park. Her next location was across the divide on land just east of Waterton National Park, Glacier's sister reserve in Alberta. Manley gave Canadian biologists her radio frequency, but no one ever located the signal again. Like her brother, Speedo, Claire cannot be counted as dead. Yet of the two, she is much more likely to have been killed—unless Speedo chose the same route—for that portion of southern Alberta is a well-known population sink for predators, an ecological black hole.

Between grizzly bear hunting seasons, legal shooting by ranchers and farmers, and the accepted use of predator poisons close to the mountains, the area around Waterton Park reveals in microcosm why the vast province of Alberta holds no more than 700 grizzlies, compared to an estimated 6,000 earlier in the twentieth century. You could argue that Alberta's grizz are in worse shape than those in the

Lower 48. British Columbia's grizzlies, meanwhile, have declined from many tens of thousands to between 10,000 and 13,000. That's the official estimate; environmental advocates and a number of scientists believe 4,000 to 5,000 is a more realistic figure. As with the Selkirk population becoming cut off on the north by development, it is a reminder that Americans might do well not to count on Canada to resupply wildlife if we run short.

There is little doubt but that Canada has been managing grizzlies in much the same cavalier way that landed the species on the threatened list in the United States. On the plus side, Canadian managers are aware of the slide and are trying harder to halt it. As one example, Alberta officials recently hired Carrie Hunt and her crew to work with problem grizzlies in the southern part of the province.

When I add the number of times that Claire and Speedo were captured and moved, first with their mother, then separately, I come up with five for him, half a dozen for her. I could also tally hundreds of hours spent tracking, watching, maneuvering, and trying to condition this family. Since we may never learn whether either of the siblings survived, it is impossible to declare the outcome a success or a bust. I know only that a strong effort was made based on science and on empathy, and that the result was days and months and years when men and women devoted more attention and care to creatures long viewed as mortal enemies than anyone would ever before have imagined. What I choose to believe is that I was witness to something new and profoundly hopeful in the history of human relationships with fellow mammals.

And if you were to ask me, I would tell you that Speedo slipped his radio collar and is living somewhere deep in the mountains next to—sure, why not?—a large, blue, fish-rippled, eminently swimmable lake. Claire's collar got cracked loose by a suitor giving her a love bite, and she is now rearing babies that look a little like Fernie. She could be doing this back in the South Fork, although my hunch is that she is way up by Jasper National Park in Alberta, having decided that if she couldn't carry her genes west to the Selkirks, she would take them north along the spine of the Rockies. No, I don't have a single fact to back up these scenarios. On the other hand, I wouldn't be the first to exaggerate a grizz tale and eventually come around to believing it to be true.

— — —

Spring almost always draws some grizz far downslope, where they move between patches of early green-up to fill bellies emptied during hibernation. That means the bear managers' months-long rest period is over as well. Although problems may mount for a while, they generally begin tapering off again as more of the uplands leaf out. In 2000, the Wind River Bear Institute's contract with the Montana Department of Fish, Wildlife & Parks ran out at the end of June. Hunt would be rehired in October, which is when the berries have frosted, shriveled, and fallen off their branches, the bears are still in hyperphagia, and troubles tend to peak again. Until then, Manley would try to keep track of Stahr in the North Fork and do a little training, though as the grizzly conflict manager for most of northwest Montana, he had a jumble of other mountainsides and valleys to cover as well.

The mother bear was more or less quiet in July. In August, Stahr led her cubs from the bottomlands up the slopes of the Whitefish Range to the old burns and avalanche tracks regrown with huckleberry brush, another being-a-good-bear kind of move. Yet by mid-September, she had descended and was poking around several of the North Fork cabins on her list of potential food sources. Along the way, she ripped boards off a garage to get at dog food kibbles packed underneath the siding by mice or bushy-tailed wood rats. Manley drove her off from a place near Coal Creek on September 25, and she went directly north to one of her favorite spots, Home Ranch Bottom.

Although the ranch owner said the grizzly wasn't getting into anything, Manley wasn't so sure, because Stahr stayed there the better part of a week. Unknown to anyone until much later, she was walking into an open barn and gorging on several hundred pounds of oats and other livestock feed. Interestingly, no one worried much about her bothering livestock during her many visits, even though Home Ranch Bottom was loaded with cows, calves, and horses. The owner had never lost a single head to grizz. This wasn't all that surprising. Despite the great bears' reputation as stock killers—and the species has produced some smashing examples—the 1,000-plus grizzlies in the Lower 48 annually take fewer than fifty cattle on average, and some years they all but boycott beef.

October 2 was the one night the man who usually slept upstairs at the Home Ranch Bottom store didn't stay there. Stahr used her new trick of ripping off boards to break into the building and grab food. She returned the next night. Manley watched her cubs padding along behind on the porch, learning the outlaw trade. He tried to catch their mother, but she eluded him and proceeded from cabin to yard up and down the valley, exactly as she had in 1998.

Hunt came back on the job about the time Stahr pulled the plywood siding off a trailer house, probably searching for more mouse-stored food. The team learned of a bird feeder she had destroyed that the owner never reported. That seemed minor after they found signs that Stahr had been ripping boards off other uninhabited buildings.

She got cat food at one place, broke into a barn at another, trashed the screen door at yet another home, scrounged cakes of horse grain from inside an unused cabin, and even broke into an outhouse. Manley and Hunt were aware that they were probably going to have to take Stahr in. She was spinning way out of control. Her fate was the continual topic of discussion as they bounced along in the pickup truck and patrolled afoot at cabin sites. The bear made the decision for them. Shortly after coming upon a veritable grizzly bear treasure chest—a freezer kept outside full of meat—she tried to get into a trailer that had people inside at the time. As Manley was soon to sum up the situation to me, "An occupied structure? That's it. She's gone."

I hadn't been keeping very close track of Stahr. I'd been watching salmon-feasting grizzlies from an observation tower at Knight Inlet on the southern British Columbia coast. I was currently home, but only long enough to pack gear for a week of hiking to follow grizzlies on the east side of Glacier Park. When I called Manley for an update, I learned that he and Hunt had caught Stahr and her offspring on October 9. They used the extralong culvert trap with two compartments and a removable panel between them, specially designed for capturing females with cubs. Since then, the grizzlies had been sitting inside it in Manley's garage. While the trio rested on fresh hay and ate apples, disoriented but oblivious to the holes they had torn in people's everyday existence, the team was calling all over the nation, seeking a home in captivity for the three bears so they wouldn't have to be put down.

Manley's house is less than three miles from where my family lives in the countryside east of Whitefish. I hurried over. The weather was chill, and the dimly lit interior of the culvert trap was misted with grizzly bear breath. Gray light fell through grated openings upon the mother and her twins, which were rustling atop the hay and grumbling to themselves. She moved about alternately dark and luminous, big and steaming and gorgeous. The cubs were big, fluffy, and golden. Both of these fuzz balls were twice the size of Stahr's surviving cub in the fall of 1998. Bright-eyed and in robust condition, they must have weighed close to 100 pounds each.

Stahr had done well by them. They were on track to become great successes in the bear world. Each deserved to be out among the mountains plying the grizzly bear trade, passing along its DNA, strengthening the population. Instead, they were uncomprehending delinquents in custody, whimpering shyly in the slanted light because their mother, in conjunction with various people, had taught them a whole suite of wrong moves.

When the bears still roamed free, Manley and Hunt and the Karelians would tell them, "No, you can't be here. You can't be doing this," and then the next human in the valley would say, "How about some garbage? Interested in a little grain?" And the cubs would look to mom, and she would say, "Don't worry. It's okay to be here. Watch, and I'll show you how to open this up." How were they to know right from wrong on their own? For that matter, it is quite possible that Stahr was only practicing behavior she had learned from her mother.

My son, Russell, who was sixteen then, had spent that summer in Utah helping to rear two hunter-orphaned grizzly cubs at Wasatch Rocky Mountain Wildlife, whose owners train bears for movies. A major part of Russell's work was simply to help socialize the pair by wrestling and cavorting with them for hours on end. Originally from Alaska, they hit 100 pounds by August, and Russell came home with interesting patterns of claw and tooth marks over most of his body. We had made a return visit to the pair before the start of his high school, where he would be a junior. Stahr's cubs reminded me of the Utah cubs almost exactly, and I kept thinking of how it had felt to have my hands deep in their fur, to smell their sweet, moist breath on my face, and to watch them romp and play-fight with my kid, who had become a young man.

The gazes of the cubs in the trap seemed unfocused, distracted, constantly alighting on different places. But I remember Stahr meeting my eyes directly as I pressed close against a small opening on top. She looked quite calm; not resigned, exactly, but poised. I wondered if that was because she was somewhat used to being held in a culvert or used to the presence of people, or both. Our eyes locked once more. I searched hard to see what I could read in those brown-irised orbs. And she spun and whanged the bejeesus out of the window and its bars so fast that I never saw what happened. I only heard the BAM! and felt the culvert vibrate. She would have taken my head off if not for the intervening thickness of metal. I had been so intent on seeing things I wanted to see that I had forgotten I was looking at a full-grown mother grizzly bear. She wasn't poor and pitiful. She was magnificent and incorrigible, and she intended to be free of us and the cylinder that held her.

Partly because the species reproduces adequately in captivity and partly because human-caused deaths in the wild leave numerous orphans to be taken in, zoos and similar display facilities have a surplus of grizz. There were no takers for Stahr and her young. Hunt was deeply discouraged.

"Even with all the structures she ripped up, everyone in the North Fork still wanted these bears kept alive," she insisted. "We found out a lot of people weren't reporting damage for fear Stahr would be taken away and killed. That worked against us all along, trying to teach her. Dammit, we had her practically being a wild bear again last year. She needed some touching up this summer, a little concentrated booster work. But there was no funding. We couldn't keep on her, and she slipped back. In five years, this is the first bear the program has dealt with extensively that has had to be put down. Look at those healthy, vibrant cubs. They have to die, and Stahr must die, because we lacked the money to maintain our position as dominant bears."

Every time Hunt looked over at the culvert trap, she saw a failure, and she was taking it personally. She believed so strongly in what she was doing that I'm not sure she could accept the fact that some individual bears, like some people, may be too hardheaded to respond to attempts to reform them. In Hunt's view, she could rehab almost every one if she could ever drum up the cash that would provide more troops with more time for each bear. I found it hard to ignore parallels to the human justice system and the endless debate between those who believe every criminal can be straightened out and those who think the solution to crime is to get tougher on the perpetrators. Not that human criminals are in any danger of vanishing from the Lower 48.

It seemed to me that wildlife officials had given Stahr all the leeway they could without abandoning their responsibilities. I thought it little short of miraculous that Montana, which is not the most liberal state in the union and ranks close to the bottom in income, was paying anyone to educate grizzlies in the first place. Once Stahr started probing buildings that had people within, the risk of disaster became intolerable, which also put the entire program to bring back the species in jeopardy. Hunt wouldn't argue with that. Yet I don't believe she personally viewed the risk of being around grizzlies in anything like normal fashion. "In our work, we have two hundred to three hundred interactions or incidents or confrontations or whatever you want to call them with grizzlies every year," she once told me, "and we've never had one where the bear showed serious aggression."

All of us devoutly wished that there really were some stretch of untamed country in the Lower 48 vast enough that Stahr's family could be dropped in the middle to carry on with their lives in wild obscurity. Such places do exist toward the northern end of the Canadian Rockies, but Canada had ceased accepting problem bears from the United States years before. Stahr couldn't be put back among the mountains. It looked as though there was no room for her beyond them either, not even with bars and a concrete floor.

Four days after the bears' capture, I was at Manley's house for a final look at Stahr's family before I took off on my high-country hike to observe her wild kin. While standing by the culvert trap, wondering as usual how these animals viewed their place in the world, I fell into a conversation with Jay Honeyman. A frequent member of the team, this Albertan had previously monitored grizzlies just east of Banff National Park. He quickly had my undivided attention as he spoke casually about what he called licking bears.

These were a couple of different young grizzlies that frequented the mountainsides near the Alberta town of Canmore. They had become so habituated to hikers that they approached people and actually sniffed, tongued, and gummed them before withdrawing. God alone knows whether the licking bears were keen to get to know the two-footed intruders better and satisfy a long-standing curiosity, thereby opening a new era of détente, or merely testing a potential food item. That grizzlies would lick and leave was astounding in itself.

After Manley joined us, I learned that a home had become available for Stahr and the cubs. The news was not cause for joy, as the family would forever be incarcerated, but it did bring a palpable sense of relief to the crew sticking around at Manley's to help out. The bears would soon be on their way to Pullman, Washington, where Charles Robbins of Washington State University would use them in studies of bear physiology and nutrition.

— — —

When you hear of an animal being packed off for experiments, part of you fears the worst. You envision the subject being poked, prodded, and maybe operated upon—tortured to some degree for the sake of knowledge. It sounded as though that was exactly what was going on as I arrived at Robbins's compound two weeks later. I knew it couldn't be, if only because a busload of schoolchildren was trooping toward the facility's cages and outdoor pens to see the grizzlies. And yet the morning air was filled with the bawling, moaning protests of suffering animals.

As it happened, that was the morning Robbins had chosen to separate Stahr from her cubs. She didn't seem terribly upset sitting apart in her new cell, but the cubs, together in theirs, were inconsolable. They were being left on their own for the first time and weaned all at once. Robbins had tried to remove them from their mother the day before I showed up, but failed. "Stahr just went ballistic," he said with a shrug. He felt that he needed to get the family separated sooner rather than later so he could feed them independently for study purposes during the prehibernation period and thereafter. The other, more practical reason was that the animals would be easier to deal with alone.

Despite the plaintive uproar from the baby bears, I enjoyed Robbins's company from the start. Tall and slender, with the fit look of a dedicated jogger, the man was plainly fond of grizz and quick to joke that he didn't take the animals down into dungeons and pry off body parts in order to analyze their threshold for pain. He explained how his work as a nutritional ecologist consisted of exposing the bears to different kinds and amounts of food and studying their growth and metabolism in nonintrusive ways.

Among other achievements, Robbins had generated seminal research into the way grizzlies fertilize ecosystems with nutrients from ocean food chains. Using isotopes to detect the marine origins of nitrogen and other key elements, he and his students measured the amounts spread around as bears dropped salmon carcasses throughout the woods and recycled the fish into urine and dung. The nutrient transfer from spawning fish to grizzly to woodland was so substantial that some trees grew 60 percent faster than normal as a result. People were starting to view the towering old-growth rainforests along the Pacific Coast partly as an expression of the spawning urges of big, hook-jawed, sea-grown fish and the appetite of grizzly bears. Ecologists even had a new term for the process: salmon trees.

Robbins and his colleagues also looked at the effects farther inland in places such as the Kenai Peninsula of Alaska. They found that between 10 and 25 percent of the growth of trees within a quarter mile of salmon stream banks was linked to bear-distributed nitrogen. Turning to museum specimens of grizzlies taken from regions such as eastern Oregon and central Idaho during the late 1800s and early 1900s, the biologists discovered that marine isotopes constituted as much as 80 percent of the major elements in their fur and bones. In other words, these interior bears too were essentially built from salmon—before they were killed off and dams wrecked the fish runs up tributaries of the mighty Columbia River. Like their counterparts along the Pacific Rim, salmon-fed grizz of grassland and sagebrush country helped promote the growth of streamside vegetation. And flourishing riparian plant communities are centers of biodiversity in such semiarid regions, being crucial to some stage in the life cycle of the majority of resident animals, from moisture-seeking amphibians and nesting birds to thirsty bobcats.

To me, this was dynamite stuff. Not only was it powerful ecology, it was one of the better answers to that perennial question: What good is a grizzly bear? Robbins also had some of the answers I was looking for concerning the behavior of Fernie and Stahr.

"I've never seen an animal so food-driven as a grizzly," he began. "A grizzly can eat one-third of its body weight per day in apples or natural fruit like berries. It can eat 15 percent of its body weight daily in meat." Naturally, I was thinking of the half ton of roadkills and heaps of apples that modest-size Fernie and her little cubs had slicked up in no time flat. "I could feed up a Rocky Mountain grizzly to 200-plus pounds—as a cub," Robbins continued. "Yet in the wild, you'll sometimes get one just 30 pounds by fall. Those cubs probably don't survive hibernation."

A stoutly reinforced exercise pen enclosing a small pasture adjoined the cage complex. Pointing to a bear rambling over the grass there, Robbins said, "A big male like Bo here will lose 150 pounds of body weight over winter—the equivalent of an average full-grown human, right? That has to be replaced. On top of it, the bear has to put on enough fat for the next winter. And on top of that, it needs energy to grow. Getting big is the key to reproductive success. For a male, it means being able to compete more successfully for mates. For a female, it translates into having more cubs at more frequent intervals and better cub survival.

"Every female grizzly wants to weigh 500 pounds, and every male 1,000. But in the Rockies, they weigh more like 300 and 500. They just can't do it on berries and pine nuts and roots. To get really big requires an abundance of animal protein and fat, and the most common source is salmon." In presettlement times, with a wealth of large, hooved animals, including an estimated 50 to 70 million bison animating the American landscape, there must have been many more plump grizz in the interior, far from salmon streams. On the Blackfeet Reservation and other portions of Montana's Rocky Mountain Front, where the bears have access to a lot of cattle carcasses among the foothills that roll onto the edge of the plains, biologists still find the occasional 700- or 800-pound male today.

Indicating a different bear, Robbins added, "I'm looking at a well-fed female with 35 percent body fat. Some salmon-eating bears in the wild are 50 percent body fat by fall. The average American is at least 25 percent body fat. Most interior grizzlies are just 17 to 18 percent. You can see why they're spending almost every waking moment trying to get food."

I could. I still didn't entirely understand why some individuals choose to go about it the troublesome way they do, while others can successfully live next to people, and still others avoid the human scene altogether. The irony was that Stahr, who devoted so much effort to trying to raid food from humans, would spend the rest of her days being fed by them after all. As for adapting to captivity, Robbins said, "She's probably the easiest bear I ever got in here." Well, she had certainly created enough opportunities over the years to become used to our two-legged presence.

Although Robbins had been emphasizing how food-driven grizzlies are, he also felt that they are strongly motivated by a desire not to be harmed. "People don't realize that a 400-pound bear can be afraid of being hurt," he said. It was a way of emphasizing that grizzly attacks are rarely predatory, but rather are part of the animals' repertoire of behavior intended to help keep them safe.

The facility we were in was once used for studying primate behavior. It still had observation windows located high above the cages by a walkway. One day, Robbins told me, a seventy-year-old faculty member was preparing to look down just as a grizzly dragged in a fifty-gallon drum from the outside yard, stood it up on end, and climbed atop the drum. That allowed the bear to reach the observation window, which it then popped open.

Aside from the elderly gentleman's shock at coming nose to nose with a grizzly bear high in the air, the surprise part of the story is that, when primates manipulated objects in that manner, it was taken as evidence of forethought—reasoning, cognitive awareness of a higher order.

One of the captive grizz I knew from Wasatch Rocky Mountain Wildlife liked to dangle chicken drumsticks outside his pen to tempt the owners' Great Pyrenees dog. When the dog came racing over, the bear would whisk the treat back inside at the last second. And yet the bear always rewarded the dog with a drumstick on its third or fourth try, as though aware that this was necessary to keep the dog's interest. Call it a bored bear figuring out ways to entertain itself. Call it a trained grizzly with its own grasp of training techniques. The Pullman bear's use of the barrel for a ladder only added to the surplus of evidence that we are a long way from really knowing what sort of animal we are dealing with here.

As I prepared to leave, Stahr was lying in her cage, half in the sheltered, concrete section and half out in the open part. She looked up with a mild expression of interest when I called to her but showed no special reaction. I took consolation in the fact that she was not pacing her quarters or bawling like her babies were. Perhaps in the years to come she would provide information that would help her kind. For the big, gilded, squalling cubs to have to spend the rest of their long lives locked up as well was an utterly dismal prospect. But I didn't know Robbins well enough to ask if he would let me drive them to, say, the foothills of California and turn them free in the old haunts of the golden bears.

FRAME OF MIND

THE LATIN LABEL given most organisms informs you that they have, say, a pronounced snout *(longirostrum)* or a yellowish fringe *(xanthimarginata)*. The grizzly's scientific name refers instead to a human opinion based upon a strong emotional reaction. In a way, that seems fitting, for this has always been a species defined less by science than by storytelling: *Ursus arctos horribilis,* horrible bear of the north.

Horror fascinates even as it repels. We invent ogres, aliens, malevolent wraiths, vampires, bugs that eat through your ear to your brain, and their ilk literally ad nauseam, as though our psyche had some sort of quota to fill. I enjoy these tales as well as the next person. As I mentioned, though, I pretty much got over the bear horrors during the course of my fieldwork on mountain goats, finding the correspondence between a grizzly's nature and ours ultimately more intriguing.

This is not to say there weren't stretches of the day and night when twigs snapped and branches trembled and shadows lurched about leaving me badly frightened. Yet each month delivered more evidence that, if grizzlies wanted to get me, they were passing up all kinds of prime opportunities. Moreover, when we did meet unexpectedly, they wheeled and bolted. They got the hell away from me as fast as they could. Why? It was a wonder, but I began to trust in it. Should one ever nail me, I felt, it wasn't going to be because grizzlies stalk around looking for such opportunities, as I had been led to believe. It would be because things went wrong.

My realigned view of the great bears also reflected my general state of mind, which was just shy of euphoric. To finally be doing hands-on wildlife research in Montana's Swan Mountains after years as a student confined to classrooms—roping goats to put radio collars on them, dodging rock falls, learning to tell shifts in the weather by smell—was immensely fulfilling. The country more than matched all the energies of a man in his early twenties, satisfied every romantic notion of mountain splendor and challenge. I came to associate much of that with grizzlies. This was the finest place I had ever lived, and it was their full-time home. How could one not admire the barons of such an estate?

Romantic notions only carry so far, though. To honestly admire any animal, you need to come to terms with all its attributes. Prominent among the grizzly's is a talent for finding and dining on amazingly foul carcasses. Each spring, grizz patrolled the bases of cliffs for the bodies of mountain goats brought down in avalanches and searched lower-elevation winter ranges for elk and deer that had failed to outlast the cold. The bears would snuggle up against the remains and lie on top of them between feeding sessions, then cache the spoils beneath dirt and debris to be unburied later and eaten in even more putrid condition.

Adult male grizzlies may kill the offspring traveling with a female, a practice observed in other apex carnivores with few natural enemies, notably wolves and big cats. This is one reason female grizzlies with young are notoriously quick to lash out at perceived threats. Yes, a cub or yearling can avoid an adult by climbing a tree trunk, because grown grizz can no longer use their long, relatively straight claws to hook into the bark well enough to support their weight. (Keep in mind, however, that big bears can clamber up trees with conveniently placed branches, more or less as a human would. I've seen full-size grizzlies fairly high in conifers, and pictures of one fifty feet off the ground in a birch canopy.) Yet because grizzlies so often choose open habitats, the tree escape route is not always handy for a youngster. Mom is. Biologically, testiness is a virtue in mother grizz.

Grizzlies usually become independent around age three, and some of those subadults may get killed by adult males. Now and then, a bear that takes down a younger one will cannibalize it. Finally, there is the ineluctable fact that, partly because of the females' defensiveness, grizzlies do attack and hurt people (about seven per year in North America during the 1990s), kill them (an average of fewer than two per year), and occasionally consume the body to boot.

This continent now holds more than 300 million *Homo sapiens* north of Mexico. In a given year, some are going to die from virtually any cause you can think of. Porch decks collapse. Tire treads separate. Doctors mix up prescriptions. Skiers hit trees. Luck turns sour, and good people expire young. Man's best friend in this vale of mixed fortune is said to be the loyal dog, genetically indistinguishable from the widely loathed and persecuted predator, the wolf. Go figure. We groom and comfort and kiss our pooches, teach them, work side-by-side with them, and address them as we would children or particularly dense adults. And every year, dog attacks send 800,000 Americans seeking medical attention—close to 5 million are bitten—and on average more than 15 to the morgue.

Vending machines that balk, then topple onto customers shaking the contraptions in frustration, cause many more injuries than bears do and, some years, more deaths. From this, we can conclude . . . what? The vicissitudes of fate are infinite, our ability to make sense of them limited, and the gap in between filled with curses and prayers. If logic offered the solace we seek, the world would have fewer lurid newspaper headlines about grizzly bear attacks and more campfire tales of narrow escapes from vending machines.

In my case, experience made a tremendous difference in relating to grizzlies. But experience hasn't changed my shark jitters one iota. When I go scuba diving, I am the soul mate of folks convinced that there is a bear behind every bush just waiting to rake them to pieces. You can remind me all day that lightning strikes or slips in bathtubs claim far more victims than all the world's sharks. It won't help. You can pass along the truly *horribilis* statistic that one of every two Americans will be in a serious automobile accident during his lifetime. When I get back in the water, I will have the mindset of people who commute to work daily in floods of traffic at seventy-five miles an hour, drive cross-country to Yellowstone National Park, and then ask if it is safe to get out of the car, what with grizzlies around.

Your conception of grizzlies is bound to be flavored by the books and movies you tasted as a child plus the last news report you saw of a gruesome mauling; by where you position humans relative to other animals in the spectrum of creation; by the moral lenses through which you view manslaughter by bears and the conscious extinction of lives by humans; by the value you place upon unfettered wilderness; by how strongly you need to feel in control and, conversely, how well you cope when vulnerable; by how you weigh the possibility of being hurt by a bear against other risks, including everyday crime, stress, drinking habits, pollutants, resistant strains of virus, and unbalanced coworkers; and by your particular quotient of the indissoluble, primal fear of being gobbled up. What would you say your quotient is? Will the part of your mind that concocts nightmares back you up on that?

My point is that, given the range of people's upbringings, personalities, inspirations, and phobias, it may not be possible to know exactly what a grizzly bear is. Every person brews up a different version from an ever changing, totally idiosyncratic mix of facts steeped in subconscious yearnings. Yet each person's image of grizzlies is equally real to him or her. Meanwhile, the bears themselves are about as different from one another in terms of habits and temperament as one human is from the next, which multiplies the variables at play.

As we've seen in earlier chapters, a mother bear passes along to her cubs a set of preferences for certain foods, habitats, and ways of responding to situations. As each of the young animals matures, it begins adding more layers of learned behavior based upon its independent experiences. Meanwhile, the bear develops a distinct home range and social rank through interactions with other grizzlies. Every adult ends up with a unique combination of such attributes, and it will have a unique personality to go with it.

Researchers who spend a good deal of time studying big, smart mammals on the order of dolphins, primates, or elephants routinely discuss their subjects' individual characters and emotional lives. This is wildlife biology with an anthropologist's slant. Although accounting for personalities seems a promising route toward understanding complex, expressive fellow creatures more fully, the scientific community is understandably wary of it. Observers are relying upon a sort of gestalt—an overall impression of the propensities and peculiarities that make an animal stand out from others. That is uncomfortably different from the analysis of hard data.

We do need to liberate natural history from the brittle, old, reductionist view of beasts as instinct-driven automatons. But we really have no agreed-upon means with which to begin. We don't even know which words to use. Where is the terminology that will let us proceed without getting tangled up in fuzzy anthropomorphism instead?

The very word *personality* is anthropomorphic. To be neutral, we ought to be talking of primatalities, elephantalities, and the like. Most everyone who has a dog is aware that his or her pet comes with a dogality, and that it is different from that of the neighbor's dog, not to mention the pent-up mutt engaged in its nightly barkathon down the street. Most dog owners also understand a dogality to be a malleable thing that can be realigned by training, by traumas, and by simple, unstinting affection. The great majority of us intuit personalities in familiar animals. We find some degree of anthropomorphism not only inevitable but helpful in relating to them. Yet the approach remains riddled with pitfalls, and as we move on to rodent-size mammals or herd dwellers, trying to interpret personalities becomes riskier yet.

So where do grizzlies fit in? For a long time, I wasn't able to observe any consistently enough to form a clear idea. Several obvious qualities bespoke the sort of behavioral plasticity and intelligence often linked with personality traits. The bears were exploratory in their ramblings and inquisitive about details. They relied upon both their strength and surprising finesse to manipulate objects in the environment. More telling for me was the role of play in the lives of these powerhouses. Young bears were devoted to it, and even the burliest adults retained a remarkable capacity for amusing themselves.

I watched loners mock-wrestle with sticks and lie on their backs to juggle logs. They would bat and bite at the edges of lake ice and make a game of pouncing on the chunks broken loose. One grown-up grizz on a summer snowfield pushed the snow around until it packed into a rough ball and rolled away downhill, at which point the bear chased after the tumbling clot and swatted it to smithereens. And, like the mother I saw glissading down a snowbank with her cubs on her lap, the bear did this over and over. Another blew bubbles in an alpine pond. Then it pricked them one by one with its four-inch-long claws. That was in huckleberry time. The living was easy, and you didn't have to know much about grizzlies to sense it. Family groups romped more than usual, and solitary bears loped in floppy mode between patches of fruit-laden bushes. If they were dogs, you would have said they were frisking; if mountain goats, gamboling.

Whereas certain grizzlies struck me as having an easygoing air about them, others seemed much less settled. Some were generally hesitant, some manifestly brash. A few appeared especially prone to suddenly display wrinkles in their muzzles, wider-than-normal eyes with white showing around the edges, and tight, jerky movements. Although I didn't know how to interpret most expressions and postures yet, my gut told me to stay well clear of the white-eyes.

During the mid-1980s, I traveled to Alaska for my first visit to a stream where grizzlies congregate to catch spawning salmon. Watching a group more or less continuously for several days amounted to a crash course in bear social behavior. I went on to more waterways thick with salmon and bears. At each site, it soon proved simpler to tell many individuals apart by their behavioral quirks than by physical appearance. I came away with little doubt that grizzly bear personalities are real, that they strongly influence the animals' interactions with their own kind and others, and that they therefore have a role in natural selection and the survival of the species.

Actually, identifying bearalities turned out to be easy. The trick was simply finding a nonthreatening, close-up situation in which to do it. Salmon spawning streams are ideal because grizzlies become more tolerant of one another in order to exploit a common bounty, and this modification of their usual fight-or-flight distance seems to carry over to people in the vicinity. Among bears habituated to human observers, you feel as if you have been given a backstage pass to go mingle with the performers.

Several times, I could have reached out and touched a passing grizzly. When one brushed my leg, I realized that I had come a very long way from my childhood encounters with imaginary bears. The real grizzlies all but ignored me. Their only acknowledgment of my presence would be to keep their eyes averted, since a stare can be a threat. Perhaps contrary to expectations, mature males are typically the bears least likely to come close to people in such settings. Mother grizzlies have figured that out. I watched females with young cubs purposefully approach people in order to use them as shields, or buffers, from big male bears moving by.

The tolerance shown by grizz at these salmon banquets extends to wolves, which go fishing more than most people suspect, to scavengers such as foxes and bald eagles, and to the occasional black bear. Grizzlies also downsize their aggressiveness in berry patches, sites with concentrations of insects, and garbage dumps—any place where food is superabundant and normal competition would prove a distraction from the feast.

In sorting out bearalities in Alaska, I began with the most obvious clue: nearly every grizzly had a different approach to catching fish. One would stand at the head of a cascade and swat at leaping salmon like a second baseman fielding grounders. The next grizz liked to sit in a pool and grasp fish that bumped against its chest. Its neighbor preferred to float like a snorkeler and claw at salmon passing below, while the grizz onshore downstream watched until a fish lingered in a back eddy, then dove onto it with outstretched paws. There were bears that chased fish thrashing through the shallows, bears that disappeared entirely underwater like chunky otters, and so on through a long and inventive list.

To be sure, a particular bear might switch techniques depending upon the kind of stream section it found itself in, and that varied as dominant bears displaced lower-ranking ones from choice spots. Even so, most of the bears continued to exhibit favorite fishing styles. When grizzlies did quarrel over rights to a fishing hole, I focused on another bearality clue: the outcome depended on more than sheer size. Assertiveness, confidence, tenacity, mettle—something in this suite of qualities played a role in success, and individuals plainly had it in different proportions. As the days passed, certain bearalities emerged as downright ornery, truly gentle, nervous, boisterous, accommodating, furtive, lighthearted, bumbling, businesslike, or borderline goofy.

The very first morning along one river, I got acquainted with a blonde I'll call Bettie. She had two cubs of the year and the softest eyes I had yet seen in a bear, meaning that hers was a very relaxed, almost heavy-lidded gaze. This was a markedly calm animal in general, whether waiting patiently in one spot to snag a fish or methodically checking on her wandering offspring rather than racing to and fro with a frantic expression, as some females with cubs in the area were inclined to do. Bettie appeared to be an experienced mother. She was also quite experienced around people. By midmorning, she was lying on her back to nurse the cubs five feet from me, so unconcerned that she seldom bothered to turn her head my way. I was sure that when she did, it would be with a warier glance than usual. No. She looked over at me with the same serene countenance.

Shortly afterward, the bear I'll call Duane showed up. He was dark and heavy, with a head like an overgrown boxer dog's. If it would sound too anthropomorphic to describe Bettie as a sweetheart, I probably shouldn't go on to say that Duane looked like he had just held up a convenience store. If nothing else, he confirmed my hunch about grizzlies with white showing in their eyes being trouble. Not that this big, tightly wound guy was out to bother me. He was a headache for other grizz, because he was, in fact, a robber.

Duane's pattern was to go from bear to bear, edging his way toward them until he could reach out and appropriate any fish they had snagged. He never barged in with a direct threat, the way a salmon thief I met elsewhere did. Duane just loitered closer and closer. Some grizzlies would keep on eating, making an effort to pretend that this male wasn't there eyeing their catch. Eventually, a Duane paw would come inching over, and maybe a single Duane claw would hook into the salmon's tail. Once that happened, the fish was as good as gone, for Duane was so large and thick and tense that none proved willing to try to back him off.

Such accounts expose the shortcomings of describing animal behavior in terms of personalities. Each one—each bearality—is a mélange easier to recognize than to explain. You find yourself relying upon terms that could hardly be less objective, and you end up compiling anecdotes rather than quantifiable, reproducible, and therefore verifiable results. In short, you haven't done science, at least not in any traditional sense. Just the same, researchers I met at viewing areas on some streams confirmed my observations and then reinforced them with a wealth of stories of their own based upon bearality traits. They also offered insights into the ways in which an individual grizzly's mood could shift. Like people, the great bears display short-term bumps and swings and flip-flops in attitude. They have bad hair days and experience longer-term adjustments as their size, social status, and repertoire of learned behavior change.

In addition to spending time among more bears on salmon streams over the years that followed, I made an effort to get to know several grizzlies in captivity fairly well. They, too, showed strong individual differences in disposition and in their willingness to experiment with new behaviors. Each owned what I would term, for want of a better phrase, an exclusive outlook on the world. Listening to trainers talk about the bearalities they worked with reminded me of parents or counselors going on about their charges' foibles and potentials.

The two Alaskan grizzly cubs that my son, Russell, helped train at Wasatch Rocky Mountain Wildlife were often given the run of a large fenced-off section of lawn with a pond. If people in the yard busied themselves entirely with the pair, Tank, a 750-pound male grizzly, would become grumbly and restless looking on from his pen. Russell's job then was to go over and soothe Tank by paying attention to him. Once, as Russell sat with his back to the pen, talking to the grown-up bear while idly chucking gravel at a can, he heard scraping sounds behind him. Moments later, he turned to find that Tank had swept together the odd bits of gravel on the pen's floor and was pushing a small pile out to him under the bottom bar with a paw.

These days, when I hear some local wildlife enthusiast declare, "You try that with a big old grizzly, he's going to . . ." or come upon the bureaucratic equivalent, "This improved management technique will cause grizzly bears to . . . ," I take it to be—at most—possibly true for part of the population part of the time. Other grizzlies are going to prove the pronouncements to be so much, well, happy horseshit, as Dad used to say.

I don't want to belabor the subject of bearalities, especially since I don't have the expertise in behavioral psychology to take it much further. Knowing a good deal more about *Ursus arctos horribilis* than I used to, I am more aware than ever of how little I know for sure, except that there is no such beast as a standard grizzly bear. Pick an image from cuddly teddy to holy terror. Some grizz, somewhere, is going to be that bear sometime. This is not tantamount to repeating the old saw about grizzlies being unpredictable. I've seen no proof that individual grizzlies are any less predictable than individual humans. Every bear has predilections and routines you can reasonably rely upon. It's mainly the variation from grizz to grizz that throws us. We're not used to ascribing nuanced personalities to huge, fierce animals that could terminate us with a casual swat.

Rather than grumble that bears don't always respond as expected, we might reexamine what it is that we have been expecting of them. Since one of the more highly developed brains in the animal kingdom lies behind the variability of grizzly behavior, we might even go on to celebrate it. Then again, we might not. You can never be sure what a human is going to do next.

Which brings up the central paradox of the grizzly's existence in the modern era. On a continent with a burgeoning human populace and shrinking wildlands, the big animals' future has come to depend mainly upon people's opinion of them. Yet we have never really been able to see the species clearly, and, to repeat the message, I'm not convinced that we can.

— ~ —

In his book *Of Wolves and Men,* Barry Lopez describes how Western cultures turned wolves into metaphors for dark apprehensions and spiritual conflicts. Projecting every sin imaginable onto the creatures—greed, gluttony, perverse desire, wanton destruction, and all the rest—Europeans mentally transformed these predators into incarnations of evil. Certainly, livestock had to be kept safe. But the vilification of wolves went so far beyond what was rationally called for that you can tell something therapeutic was going on. Something like an attempt to purge the devil people feared within themselves. Something like a subconscious effort to keep at bay those forces always gnawing at our inhibitions, always tempting, always circling out there at the firelight's edge, whispering pagan enticements. Or maybe something far older, having to do with the origins and purpose of destructive compulsions during hominid evolution. I have a feeling that if we grasped more of what went into such exorbitant hatred of an animal competitor, we could make better sense of conundrums like the Spanish Inquisition or apartheid, but I don't want to detour that far.

Native Americans have a wealth of favorite grizzly bear stories narrated through the centuries. An example would be the tale that Lakota Sioux told of the silvertip Hu Nanpa—Two Legs—who argued with a moose over who would be chief of the animals, or the advice given Blackfeet warriors by Real Bear during a vision quest. In European American culture, the great bear legend passed along from elder to young goes something like this: The guy put round after round into the hulking brute. And still, still, O God, still it kept coming. Just when he could almost feel its hot breath on his face, he fired his last bullet . . . and the grizzly dropped dead at his feet.

To a large extent, the origins of the classic tale can be traced back to 1806, when the Lewis and Clark expedition returned from the far reaches of the Louisiana Purchase. Among the highlights of their discoveries were huge "grisled," or piebald, bears that couldn't be laid low with one bullet—or, at times, even with three or four. The party shot more than two score of the novel beasts anyway, primarily out of curiosity and to collect additional specimens.

An assault with low-velocity rounds from a black powder rifle that requires reloading after every blast is an extremely effective way to turn a wandering silvertipped bear into the engine of wrath in a mighty outback drama. The men who ventured west after Lewis and Clark confirmed this time and again. The legend grew. Grizz became the favorite monsters of America's seemingly boundless, still largely mysterious frontier.

After livestock was herded into the new territory, the grizzly took on some of the wolf's moral burden as a symbol of depravity. Both were portrayed as leering abominations that gutted livestock for the sheer joy of wreaking havoc, taunting the efforts of settlers striving to impose order on a savage domain. But to the public at large, the grizzled bear remained first and foremost the gigantic man-ripper that just keeps coming—a hairy New World dragon.

You slay dragons because it's the right thing to do, virtually a public service. And of course, the deadlier a dragon is made out to be, the more valiant the knight seems who confronts it. This tradition continued straight through to my childhood, when every second cover on those sportsmen's magazines in my room depicted an enraged grizzly looming high over a man and his gun.

Bears have to die so the legend may live. Montana and Wyoming continued to sell an unlimited number of grizzly hunting licenses right up until 1975, when so few of the bears remained south of

Canada that the species was listed as threatened. Trophy hunting of grizzlies and other varieties of the brown bear, *Ursus arctos,* persists as a multimillion-dollar industry today in Alaska, Canada, northern Europe, Siberia, and Russia's Far East.

Big bears can be tough to knock down even with the latest sporting rifles and ammunition. Although a kill doesn't usually play out all that dramatically, it can still serve to validate a man who would be known as brave. When you hear a shooting-the-grizzly tale, old or new, you quickly find yourself swept up in the bellowing and charging and desperate, last-second moves. And—just as with the Lewis and Clark accounts—that's what people remember as the heart of the saga: the grizzly attacking and the human defending, not that a human attacked first with bullets and provoked a bear to defend itself the only way it knows how. Endlessly repeated, the legend is thus one of the chief reasons much of the public continues to believe there is a high probability of a grizzly going after a person when it sees one.

However, with the revolution in ecological awareness during the latter half of the twentieth century, modern America spawned a second myth. In this one, the once indomitable grizzly has become the vulnerable, even fragile, essence of the last wilderness redoubts. I've written about the species that way myself, not quite aware that I wasn't describing the animals themselves so much as the importance of wildlands and the freedom found therein to me.

In the revisionist legend, the grizzly once more joins the wolf, for both are presented as creatures too attuned to untamed rhythms, too purely wild, to withstand the hurdy-gurdy of progress. The role of ravagers of beauty and despoilers of harmony gets assigned to humans. Justice moves over to stand on the besieged predators' side. I can remember when, during the early 1970s, demonic magazine-cover grizz began competing with hippie grizz—poster images of a peaceful-looking bear in an alpine setting above a phrase from a Beatles song: Let It Be.

Along those lines, grizzlies have been used to symbolize the rugged grandeur of the mountain West and North to such an extent that many people assume the great bears inherently prefer such landscapes. They don't. They were doing fine on the Great Plains in places like Saskatchewan and Kansas until they got shot and trapped and poisoned out. They liked the California coast and its chaparral hills and roamed the Sonoran desert contours of Arizona. More inhabited a broad swath of northern Mexico. Hunters took at least four still holed up in the Sierra del Nido range of Chihuahua toward the end of the 1960s.

To define grizzlies as a sensitive wilderness species or dependent upon pristine habitats is also confusing. As with most popular images of the bears, it doesn't tell you what they are intrinsically like, only that people have been lethally intolerant of them outside protected or relatively inaccessible areas. Granted, some grizz can't handle much human disturbance. But plenty would live in suburban yards, cornfields, and smoldering municipal dumps if we let them.

I've come across grizzlies that bounded away in utter dismay from low-flying helicopters, and grizzlies that reared up raging to swat the air as the whirlybirds passed; silvertips that sought out cattle to kill, silvertips that shared pastures and even mineral licks with herds, and silvertips that fled from gangs of bossy cows; great bears that turned back upon discovering the scent of a human's tracks in the wild, great bears that strolled the streets and yards of my hometown, and one mother bear that took to camping with her cubs under the steel girders of a drilling rig lying on its side in Alaska's Prudhoe Bay oilfield. That female's sister walked through a machine shop in broad daylight and snatched a busy worker's lunch so deftly that when he turned around and noticed it missing, he started cussing his coworkers, accusing them of the theft. Another grizz in the area used to climb three stories on the fire escape on the outside of a roaring, steam-belching factory building to snooze in the breeze up there, blissfully free of mosquitoes.

— — —

Brown bears are one of the most widely distributed of modern species.

Among large carnivores, only the wolf claims a broader geographic distribution, and *Homo sapiens* is the only large land-based mammal with a total range exceeding that of the wolf. The key is adaptability. All three of us are experts at high-grading the food supply across a wide assortment of plant communities and topography.

In regard to territoriality, cooperative hunting, and an extended family social structure, wolves and humans are strikingly similar. The bears occupy general home ranges instead of defending specific territories, and the basic family unit is limited to a mother and cubs that usually disperse well before they mature. However, that doesn't mean grizzlies without cubs are always loners on the prowl, as popular accounts imply. A good number are periodically gregarious in relation to food bonanzas.

Along with the hot spots for berries, insects, and salmon mentioned earlier, cutthroat-trout spawning streams bring grizzlies together. So do sites where carcasses have collected from a die-off. Stories of shouts, shots, and hair's breadth escapes piled up fast when the Lewis and Clark party made it up the Missouri River to Great Falls, Montana. The shores turned out to be prickly with grizz scavenging the remains of a bison herd that apparently had fallen through the ice upstream in winter. Long before that, Spanish explorers discovered lodes of California's golden grizzlies dining together on beached whales. As more grizzlies are fitted with radio collars, researchers find some associations between mothers and cubs lasting longer than expected. Once the siblings leave, they occasionally stay bonded to each other for another couple of years, denning together as young adults. In a few cases, the radio signals show fully grown female relatives continuing to either share a home range or occupy strongly overlapping ranges, even when both have cubs of their own.

In the end, then, it is not the grizzly's habitat requirements or its social behavior that truly separate this species from every other we might encounter within the same countryside. It is the characteristic that we don't know what to do about: raw, overwhelming power.

Despite all efforts to horribilize them, despite the fact that the vast majority of grizzlies in the tales we tell each other are presented as terrorists, grizz rarely live up to that image. But they are never to be trifled with and never to be ignored. Afield, you have to acknowledge their existence. And you need to do this at every level of being, from your train of thought to your listening and sniffing, to that intangible sixth sense of what waits around the next bend.

A grizzly commands attention merely by being in the same zip code. It elicits respect and enforces a measure of humility. None of these is a condition easily instilled in Americans. Some folks resent the bears precisely for requiring this magnitude of awareness outdoors. A good deal of what we mean when we complain that grizzlies are unpredictable is that they are not subject to us. They can be killed and even locally exterminated, but they cannot be made to accept our reign. Whose woods are these, anyway? Whose mountainsides? That this should be a point of contention between us and any animal is an affront to some people's sense of the world's design. It offends their basic notion of human purpose.

Attention, respect, humility: these are elements of homage, something we ordinarily reserve for gods, heroes, and maybe a lover or two. It wasn't always so. Or maybe it would be more accurate to say that definitions of gods have changed. Paleolithic human remains appear to have been ceremonially buried with arrangements of bear parts. From these, authorities speculate that the Ice Age European cave bear, *Ursus spelaeus,* as well as the brown bear, had spiritual or totemic significance for early people. Worship of the brown bear continued as a central feature of the Ainu culture on the northern Japanese island of Hokkaido until fairly recently. An argument could be made that the cult of the great bear constitutes humankind's oldest, most enduring religion.

Short-faced bears, which preceded the *Ursus* line, were even larger, rangier, and more strictly predatory. They would have been formidable enough to perhaps keep human groups from successfully colonizing some regions altogether. Whatever the case, even where great bears didn't double as shaggy deities, they surely held people's imaginations in thrall.

After Paleo-Indians joined grizzlies in the New World, the two arrived at a sort of equilibrium. In their traditional tales, native Americans refer to other creatures as relatives: brother, grandfather, cousin. They speak of animal tribes, calling them the wolf people, fish people, mosquito people, and so forth. Many clans claim descent from the more potent, heraldic species among them, including great bears.

I'm only describing a framework of culturally binding beliefs. It's not for me to guess to what extent people actually considered stories of direct kinship with animals to be grounded in fact. I'm not an indigenous American. The relationship between facts and faith in my own culture is an enigma. This much is probably fair to assume: whereas Westerners have gone to considerable philosophic lengths to separate themselves from the rest of creation, native Americans did the opposite. In most of their cosmologies, all living things possessed a spirit. Neither higher nor lower than other organisms, humans were one more form making up the sacred circle of existence.

Another reason natives could not conceive of North America's fauna in anything like modern fashion is that (with the exception of the dog and, later, the horse) all animals were untamed. People had no reason to think of a creature as wild or of a setting as wilderness. They thought of them as the world.

Native Americans and grizzlies were essentially codominant across much of the continent. By the same token, when members of modern American society venture into what remains of grizzly country, the clear supremacy that most take for granted becomes open to dispute. If you enjoy looking down on the pyramid of life from its very pinnacle, if you like to lounge alone and sovereign at the end of the food chain, you might want to consider going somewhere else. Where grizz endure, you are part of the ecosystem, whether you believe you are or not. You are in nature, the way people used to be. It's enough to make you lose your swagger out there. For some, that will be upsetting; for others, an opportunity to reconnect.

THE GRIZZ
FROM LACY LANE, EASY STREET, AND DAKOTA AVENUE

WHITEFISH, MONTANA, population 5,000, lies at the foot of Big Mountain, the southern terminus of the Whitefish Range. During the fall of 1999, the local paper reported that a resident wending his way home after an evening on the town met a grizzly along Wisconsin Avenue, one of the main streets. The man said that the bear ran after him for several blocks, and he thanked his lucky stars that he had been able to keep ahead of it.

I looked closely at the accompanying picture. The fellow was not young, and he was a world away from trim. Since the average *Ursus arctos horribilis* can outsprint a racehorse, I put the incident down in my notebook as a dandy grizz tale, meaning that a more accurate rendering of the facts would only have spoiled it. I didn't doubt the part about encountering a grizz, though. Whitefish was hosting at least half a dozen that autumn. The one in the story was probably Lacy.

The bear's pattern had been to come down off the side of Big Mountain at night to plunder apples from yards on the north end of town, mostly between Wisconsin Avenue and the shore of Whitefish Lake. Erik Wenum of the wildlife department caught this female along Lacy Lane and deported her about fifty miles north into the

Whitefish Range. She returned for more apples within a week. From that point on, Lacy's urban life was literally dogged by the bear conflict management team of Tim Manley, Carrie Hunt, their assistants, and assorted Karelians.

Unlike the hefty fellow who made the news, motorists, bicyclists, and the odd jogger went by oblivious to the large, wild omnivore picking fruit in the streetlights' shadows. Manley remembers watching an unsuspecting newspaper boy make his predawn rounds past a house where Lacy was at work in the backyard.

That people were generally unaware of a grizzly in such close proximity didn't strike Manley as too remarkable, nor did the fact that the bear pretty much ignored them. He was around such situations all the time. What surprised him was how little attention anyone paid to a band of people with guns and dogs stalking through neighborhoods in the wee hours. If they had been the wrong kind of commandos, Whitefish would have fallen under their control with scarcely a peep. Maybe passersby figured them for hunters returning late from the woods. Manley finally managed to shoot Lacy in the open with a drug-laden dart and relocate her to the North Fork. A few days later, he free-ranged her in Whitefish again. She was twenty feet from the boat dock on City Beach.

The north end of Whitefish proper has been steadily pushing up against the southern foot of Big Mountain for years, and condos and trophy homes keep popping up higher on the slopes. Although the upper elevations are principally national forest land, a good portion of the federal acreage overlooking town was leased decades ago for development as a ski resort. Big Mountain now boasts a terrific array of runs. It is also traditional feeding habitat for grizzlies, and some hibernate not far from the groomed slopes and chairlifts. Because the resort is on federal property, it has the distinction of being required to shut down in early April, even when plenty of skiable snow remains, to avoid disturbing bears during the critical period when they emerge from their dens with depleted energy reserves and their metabolism not yet fully up to speed.

Recreation resumes at Big Mountain once summer begins. A favorite activity is to take the lift to the summit and hike down the face. The previous year, Manley and Hunt had been called in to deal with a grizzly feeding close to a popular trail. They trapped the animal—a small, newly independent two-year-old female—near the ski run known as Easy Street and removed her to a quieter portion of Big Mountain. Easy, as she was known from then on, kept returning to the busy south face. So did the team, working with the dogs to shoo her away and get the message into her young head that the townward-facing slope was off-limits.

In 1999, Easy, like many grizz, descended from her den site to graze early grass shoots flush with the nutrients that had been stored over winter in the roots. Unfortunately, the grass she chose was in the yard of a Big Mountain condo. She traveled farther downhill to a golf course—eighteen holes' worth of solid, sprouting, well-fertilized meadow. Relocated yet again, she found her way back to Big Mountain. This time, she kept off the main slope, and as a greater variety of vegetation sprouted, she began frequenting more remote sections of the southern Whitefish Range.

Another female grizzly drawn to Whitefish in 1999 appeared in autumn, going after apples. Manley figured her for one of the several grizz that had found food in Whitefish the previous fall. This time, she got a name, Dakota, for she was captured on Dakota Avenue on the city's north side. The bear was radio-collared and sent to Whale Creek, which drains east off the Whitefish Range into the North Fork. Upon her release, she received the full negative treatment: people drumming on the steel culvert trap and Karelians barking like mad on all sides, followed by stinging rubber bullets as she made her getaway. Dakota hightailed it north to Trail Creek, just a few miles from the Canadian line, and disappeared a few weeks later into a high-country winter den.

In the spring of 2000, Lacy and Easy were on the southwest side of Big Mountain. Each was grazing lawns. Both had discovered that the bird feeders in those yards were full of edibles too. The bears were relocated to the upper North Fork. Lacy came back south and was in and out of trouble for days. As the last snow patches dissolved into green shoots and leaves, Lacy began leading a quieter existence, occasionally showing up near human habitation but feeding primarily on natural foods. She worked her way around to the back side of Teakettle Mountain near the Flathead Valley town of Columbia Falls. And it was there that a sportsman from South Dakota shot her during Montana's spring black bear hunting season. The guy returned to town crowing about the really nice, big black bear he had bagged. He genuinely did not have a clue as to what kind of animal he had felled.

Easy stuck around the North Fork. The team worked her a few times to encourage her to avoid homesites there. She turned to the backcountry and roamed at least ten miles into Canada. As summer wore out and fall colors took over, she was quietly eating berries back in the United States. With the onset of winter, she denned in the Ten Lakes area on the far western side of the Whitefish Range.

Dakota's spring travels in 2000 took her to the North Fork home of the photographer who had attracted so many other grizzlies over the years. The man had since moved away, and the place was clean, so it looked as though Dakota was visiting because she remembered getting easy food there in previous years. The bear team thought this might have been how she originally went astray. They gave her a few sessions of instruction via guns and dogs, hoping to turn any positive association with the place into a negative one. She fled and passed a good part of the summer in Glacier Park and just across the river, in the bottomlands around my cabin. As soon as the huckleberries ripened, she went west, traveling upslope on national forest land in the Whitefish Range to Cyclone Peak.

Everyone in Montana has a theory about what makes some places better than others, and some years better than others, when it comes to producing "hucks." Whatever the factors are that make *Vaccinium* bushes happy, Cyclone is well endowed with them; even in an ordinary year, the whole mountain has a huckleberry tang. My wife, Karen, worked several summers as the fire lookout in the tower atop

Cyclone and gorged on these tart, wild relatives of the blueberry while going and coming on the trail. She also stepped over impressive piles of bear dung en route, for the peak always attracted grizz. In Dakota's case, Cyclone made a major contribution to her fall weight, and she went on to den higher up near the Whitefish Divide.

As usual, the team couldn't claim that their strategy of close monitoring and aversive conditioning had proved to be a cure-all for bears with a history of misbehavior. There was evidence of rehabilitation in some of the bears the team had been trying to teach, but the unqualified success took place down on the bottom line. That was where you counted the grizzlies, notably the reproducing or soon-to-be-breeding-age females, that were still alive.

— — —

As the weather warmed in 2001, Easy reappeared northeast of Eureka, Montana, close to the Canadian line. She had come down into the Tobacco Valley, which, together with the Stillwater River Valley farther south, separates the Whitefish Range from the less rugged Salish Mountains to the west. Swinging south, she arrived at a ranch and found dog food and garbage on the porch of the main house. The outfit ran sheep and had experienced problems with wolves after a pack of the endangered carnivores established a territory in the area. Knowing that the stockman had been pissed off about feeding one recovering predator species already, Manley hurried to set up a trap and get Easy out of everyone's hair. In the process, he discovered that the stockman had recently passed away. "His wife turned out to be a sweet woman, a pleasure to deal with," Manley told me. "Her comment was, 'What a beautiful bear.'"

Easy avoided the trap and continued south past the little community of Stryker to a still smaller outpost called Radnor. At two o'clock in the morning, Manley got a telephone call from a combination trailer court and rural subdivision complaining about a grizzly raiding dog food from a porch. Manley said to just make noise and chase the bear off, adding that he would be there first thing in the morning. He made good on his word, and he tried in vain for hours to free-range the female. In the end, he settled for putting out a culvert trap and snares, then drove home to the Flathead Valley. It was his birthday. He had a party planned for that evening. His hopes of being around for all of it were not high.

"Seems like I've had a bear call in the middle of my birthday about every year since I started this job," Manley said. He was shopping for party supplies at a Wal-Mart when his mobile phone rang. Easy had stepped into one of his snares. Determined to salvage something of the evening's plans, he dashed to his house, rounded up the guests, and took everybody along with him to Radnor. Since a good half of them were involved in wildlife work anyway, it didn't seem an unreasonable way to socialize.

Suppose a neighbor rang you up in the early hours, gasping something about a grizz just outside his door. A version of the night-roaming hulk instantly rears up in your mind. How large? After tranquilizing Easy, Manley recorded her spring weight. It was 210 pounds. The female was as small in stature as she was unaggressive. This was why he had felt comfortable telling the Radnor homeowner to simply scare the bear off the porch. "The name Easy fits her," he told me. "She's a very easygoing, mellow bear." After transferring her into a mobile culvert trap, he led his friends back home and finished celebrating his birthday.

The grizzly was turned loose close to the Canadian border in the North Fork. Five days later, she was in the same Radnor subdivision, eating dog food off the same porch, the owners having sort of forgotten to get around to cleaning things up. Before Manley could catch her again, she moved a short distance south to Olney and caused a stir as she checked that little community out. Before anyone got too riled, the bear continued toward Big Mountain. She lingered there for the remainder of the spring in acceptably anonymous fashion, keeping to herself in the woods.

Easy had been caught and moved five times in all, two more than the three-strikes-and-you're-out rule allows. But Manley had been revising the strike zone, so to speak. "The state and the feds are still leery of exceeding the limit, and that's understandable," he told me. "My position is: Let's look at this individual. She grew up on Big Mountain. It's her home. Why should it count as a strike if we catch her eating bird food where people just moved in?"

On the 27th of June 2001, I hopped into Manley's pickup, the dust-caked, dinged-up camper behind the cab as familiar by now as the rattle of loose gear inside. He had backed the rig into so many overhanging branches trying to turn around on narrow mountain roads late at night that the metal shell had more odd angles than straight lines. I could see four or five fresh dents and holes in the peeling aluminum skin. This had become a mere carcass of a camper. Like the road-killed game so often tossed onto its floor, it seemed to be rotting before my eyes.

As usual, dog noises were emanating from the thing, Manley having kept some Karelians after Carrie Hunt left for the summer. However, I noticed that the number of barks per minute was substantially higher than usual. This turned out to be due entirely to the addition of a young female named Blush. All the dogs were given to barking if we passed the scent of wildlife, particularly bears. Blush, however, barked through the middle of town. Blush barked at gas stations and parking lots. Blush barked at the sky. She barked because she was excited to be in a vehicle bound for adventures unknown, and her celebration went on without letup wherever we went.

Manley made a perfunctory check for different bears' radio frequencies as we drove, but Easy's was the one he really wanted to pursue. Not that she had sparked any midnight phone calls to the bear educator's house lately. On the contrary, it looked as though she was still using all the right parts of Big Mountain and avoiding the developed south face, being good as gold. It was just that Manley hadn't been able to fly and pinpoint locations from the air for a while. He needed to reassure himself that the ground-based signals he had been picking up from Easy weren't bouncing around and misleading him somehow.

We came to the guard station for a new, gated luxury subdivision on the lower portion of Big Mountain's south face. Considering the decomposed state of the rig we were in, the attendant must have had second thoughts about letting us pass. Manley stuck his head out the window and began chatting in his straightforward style. He no sooner mentioned getting a better fix on footloose grizzlies than we were ushered straight through with an encouraging wave.

The subdivision's new golf course was one of two that Easy had previously explored. But as we looped by the greens and elegant new homes, her radio location stayed distant. The signal was coming from farther upslope or spilling over from the mountain's backside; it was hard to tell which. We drove on to the base of the ski hill and, to Blush's chagrin, took only a radio receiver and antenna with us for a chairlift ride.

From the summit, a few sweeps of the antenna determined that Easy was on the opposite side of the mountain from town. Slower sweeps and some fine-tuning of the receiver put her near the course of a creek down a side valley. The location suggested that she was in a typical early summer pattern of feeding, concentrating on streamside plants such as crisp, celery-like cow parsnip stems, which kept her out of view in thick cover. Perfect.

A silver-tipped group of retirement-age tourists was traipsing about the summit at the time. When the naturalist leading them prevailed upon Manley to give an impromptu talk on radio telemetry and grizzly ecology, I slipped into the restaurant for a little summit shopping. Bearing juices and snacks, I rejoined Manley, and we rode a gondola back down the mountain, winding up the most civilized stint of alpine grizzly bear tracking I had done in some time.

— — —

The last day of August, Manley called and asked if I wanted to ride up the Stillwater Valley with him. He was going to Stryker, the small roadside settlement about forty miles northwest of Whitefish and eight miles south of Trego. The purpose was to investigate the first call he had received about a grizzly problem anywhere in the Flathead watershed since the 24th of July. Although 2001 was proving to be a below-average year for huckleberries, it was by no means a bust like 1998. Manley's take on the current conditions was, "There are enough good patches around if you know where to find them, and if you're a bear, you do."

The grizzly roaming Stryker was Dakota. She was leading two cubs of the year. As in 2000, she had passed much of the summer in and around the North Fork bottomlands, often in the vicinity of

DAKOTA'S WHEREABOUTS, FALL 1999 TO FALL 2002

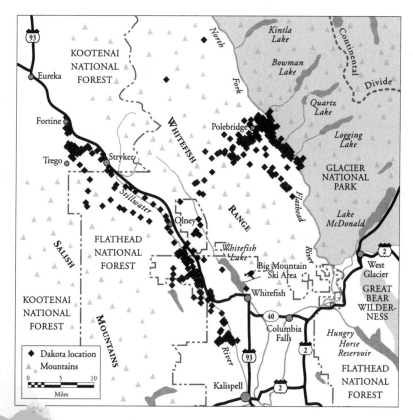

Karen's and my property. As soon as the huckleberries came on in mid-August, this bear once again moved up to Cyclone Peak. She and the cubs were following their noses from patch to fruited patch there when a thunderstorm swept through.

Montana was in its fourth year of serious drought. Scarcely a drop of rain had fallen since spring. The woods felt kiln-dried, the moisture content of their plants and soils measuring as low as anyone could remember. Lightning struck a high slope of the Whitefish Range, and the spot lit like tinder. Suddenly, the grizzly family was fleeing for their lives from a wildfire rolling across tens of thousands of acres.

Manley would later investigate the remains of a female grizzly found in the blaze's path. Probably choking on smoke and badly disoriented, its keen sense of smell useless for finding the way, the animal had burned to death when strong prevailing winds from the west carried the inferno down from the ridgelines. The flames roared on through the national forest and soon swept into the park, jumping the wide North Fork River as if it didn't exist. Dakota's family escaped by circling westward around the blaze. They didn't stop until they reached the Stillwater Valley, abandoning the Whitefish Range altogether.

The huckleberries were sparse in the bottomlands, but then they usually were. On the other hand, serviceberries, chokecherries, and hawthorn berries hung in succulent profusion. If anything, the overall crop of wild fruits was better in the valleys than at higher elevations that year, so the forced move wasn't too hard on the bear family in terms of nutrition. The downside lay in the number of people the bears now found themselves dining next to.

Manley's call had come from Tim Thier, a wildlife department colleague based in the Stillwater Valley. Thier passed along the news that the three grizzlies had bedded down the previous night on the shore of Dickey Lake, about twenty yards from eighty kids and twenty adults at a Bible camp. It sounded like a recipe for panic. "I guess a couple of the old-timers were a little wary," Manley said. "But on the whole, nobody was too concerned." He shrugged, as if to emphasize that, while you can sometimes judge how a grizzly will respond to a given set of events, people will endlessly surprise you.

While Manley tooled along Highway 93 in that direction, we passed a series of garbage Dumpsters lined up in a pullout on the shoulder—the closest thing to a refuse collection service in the rural Stillwater Valley. "We got the old bins replaced with bear-proof models two years ago," he noted. With urging from his department, the same switch had been made voluntarily by the Big Mountain ski resort and by the new luxury subdivision we had visited. And the city of Whitefish recently passed a bear-conscious ordinance requiring residents to wait until the morning before setting household garbage out on the edge of a street for collection.

Step-by-step, acre-by-acre, people were responding to the fact that great bears were no longer sliding toward extinction and the place promised to be grizzly country for some time to come. Put another way, humans and silvertips alike were slowly, haltingly, yet perceptibly, refining the art of living on common territory in northwestern Montana.

For her part, Dakota had never yet taken anything other than fruit from around human dwellings, at least not as far as Manley knew. We reached Stryker around eight in the morning. Homing in on the collared female's signal, we followed a dirt road past a scattering of houses separated by the railroad line that runs through the valley. Where we crossed the tracks, we could see some distance along the raised railroad bed. And there was Dakota with the two cubs, sauntering down the center like hoboes on a stroll.

Manley turned around and drove to a house close by that section of tracks. He grabbed a gun and his pepper spray, leashed a couple of dogs to his waist and one to mine, and led the way up the steep berm to the tracks. The grizzlies were gone, leaving us among the cinders with a fresh deposit of dung full of berry pulp and seeds.

No one answered at the house when Manley knocked at the door. Several full bird feeders hung from the eaves and nearby posts. We could see where the grizz trio had explored the yard and its little pond, but none of them had touched a feeder. The additional droppings we found held only more recycled berries from bushes like those fringing the lawn. Manley scribbled a note about the bears, with a suggestion to empty the bird feeders until winter. He clipped it to the door, and we headed for the home of a woman named Helen, who had reported grizzlies roaming her property.

Harkening back to the visits by Fernie and Stahr to the homes of single women, Manley had informed me that Helen was a widow living on her own. I began to wonder whether mother bears preferred the houses of solitary human females or Montana menfolk just didn't last very long. As we looked over the setting, taking in the lawn, its inevitable bird feeders, the Stillwater River and its serviceberry brush on the yard's west side, plus a prodigiously fruited chokecherry right next to the house, the woman emerged from the front door.

Manley said, "Hi Helen," as if he had known her for years. Actually, he had, not from travels through rural communities to carry out bear management but because he had once lived in Stryker himself. In a community that size, you could meet everyone within a couple of hours. Manley had been there several years. In talking with his old neighbor, Manley ascertained that Dakota and the cubs had been regulars in the area the past few days. The woman wouldn't have called to complain, she told us, except she believed that two sets of grizzly mothers with twins were hanging around, one female being markedly darker and larger than the other.

Manley mentioned that the same grizzly can look much different at different times, depending upon the way the light hits its fur. Although Helen politely agreed, she was plainly far from convinced. Three, six, whatever the number of grizz nearby, she was happy to let Manley set out a baited culvert trap for them on her property. If he put it at the far end of her yard, the action would be no more than 150 yards from her front window, he warned her. She didn't have a problem with that either. By the time the two were finished talking things over, Manley had volunteered her to keep an eye on the trap so she could call right away if any of the bears went in. He reemphasized that anything can happen when you're trying to catch a whole family, particularly if one of the cubs gets caught and momma grizz is still outside, running around supercharged with anger and fear.

Helen raised her eyebrows and told him, "Go ahead. I'll miss church this morning, but I guess that will be all right."

We offloaded the culvert trap, then went back to the railroad line and drove down the maintenance road next to the tracks, taking readings with the radio antenna. I spotted three bears about 170 yards off. They were at the edge of a clearing between Helen's place and the first house we had visited.

At first, even Manley was taken aback by how dark the grizzly appeared to be—too dark to be Dakota. "Has to be the angle she's at," he muttered. "Dakota has a really light face, a lot of silver on that part. Come on, turn. Ah. There's our girl." She had swung our direction, and her head was now bright as a panda's. No wonder Helen was so insistent about there being two distinct females around. The cubs were lighter overall, with a white ring running around the chest and shoulders of each, as is often the case for young grizz. Yet they too assumed alternating shades from platinum to dusky as they moved. It was as though we were slipping polarizing sunglasses on and off our eyes.

"Hey bear, go on! Hey Bear! GO ON!"

Until Manley yelled out the window, Dakota hadn't paid the least attention to us, though she had to have heard the sound of the truck alongside the tracks. Abruptly, she lifted her head and looked directly our way. An instant later, she was loping into the adjoining woods like a scolded dog. "She's one of those bears," Manley noted. "That's all you have to do, and she'll move right off every time. I imagine a lot of people wish their pets responded that well."

It was time to bait the trap, but Manley didn't want to use meat. For one thing, Dakota had never been rewarded with that kind of food near human settlements, and he didn't want to risk teaching her to make such a link. Second, although Stryker was less a town than a loose collection of homes in the forest, the populace included enough dogs that one would likely come in to a meat scent and trigger the trap—if Helen's own dog didn't get there first. Which is why we drove to the Trego Mercantile, picked up an onion sack that the proprietor had saved for Manley, and filled it with apples from the overloaded trees behind the store. At Helen's, we mashed a few fruits to bring out the aroma, dumped the pile into the culvert, and set the trigger linked to the bait pan.

Manley walked over to talk some more with the woman, who had come out to watch the proceedings from a distance. She was in her sixties or possibly older, small and silver haired. You could fairly describe her as slightly frail physically, but she had the unflinching air of someone who had long relied on herself with satisfactory results. This was a weather-resistant Montanan more than ready for whatever came next into her neck of the woods. She'd once had a black bear messing around her back porch, she told us. It wouldn't budge when she yelled at it, and when she made a move to shoo it away, the animal charged the door instead. Her dog distracted it long enough for Helen to grab a metal-handled broom. She had no intention of using it for defense. Her plan was to give the bear a thrashing.

"I fought around with that crazy bear for quite a while there," she recalled. "I got in a good whack on its head, but it wouldn't go away. Then I thought: I'll go get my pistol and fire some shots; you know, in the dirt right by it. Well, I fired two, and the bear never blinked an eye. Later, it did move off a little. But then it came right back to the porch. The dog went after it again, and we fought around with that crazy bear some more . . ." Until, presumably, it grew deeply discouraged and left; she never bothered to say.

Dakota and her cubs avoided the trap and went south from Stryker to Trego and then north to Fortine, yet another tiny community in the valley. She ambled by bird feeders, garbage cans, and other household enticements without helping herself to any. The bear family even passed by apple trees, content to stick to the wild fruits.

What, then, was the attraction of the scattered towns, which Dakota consistently seemed to seek out? Were the berries so much better around settled parts of the bottomland? Was this mother bear getting into human provisions we didn't know about? Manley examined more than two dozen droppings left in her wake. None held anything but berry residue. I wondered if, like females at salmon streams, Dakota was using the presence of humans as a sort of buffer against larger, more dominant yet warier bears, notably males that might threaten the cubs. The only other explanation I could think of was that, despite having undergone some limited aversive conditioning, she rather enjoyed the stimulation of being near people and their activities. Maybe she found us interesting.

As conspicuous as Dakota insisted upon keeping herself, she had half the valley gossiping about a mother grizzly with cubs running around. Manley made his standard effort to provide details to as many residents as he reasonably could while out tracking. Typically, some folks shrugged, some were secretly tickled by the extra excitement, and others rumbled about getting rid of the damn things the old-fashioned way. Advances in learning to live with great bears notwithstanding, it remains easy to find Montanans who live on Silvertip Lane, shop at Great Bear Grocery, dine at the Hungry Bear Cafe, drink at the Grizzly Den, ride a Grizz XK5000 snowmobile, buy their truck's tires at Grizzly Auto, and despise actual grizzly bears, either because they are afraid of them or because they see the animals as symbols of egregious federal regulations, or both.

Another single woman in the area who found a female grizzly by her home that fall responded by firing her rifle. She aimed over the animal's head to frighten it, she insisted, and the bear ran off immediately afterward. But the body was later found 100 yards away in a creek bed. She had hit it dead on in the side.

～ ～ ～

On the 20th of September, I checked my telephone answering machine to find the following message: "Hi. This is Tim with your daily grizzly report." Manley updated the histories of a handful of bears we had tracked together, concluding with, "I've got Dakota and the cubs over here at my place if you want to come by and say hello."

I did. Manley described free-ranging all three and began to contemplate their options for the future aloud. Our discussion meandered for a bit, rambling over a variety of subjects before the lightbulb went on in my head.

"You've sure been saying nice things about me today," I observed.

"Well gosh, it must be because you're such a wonderful person."

"Right. You want to dump these grizzly bears on our place in the North Fork, don't you."

"It would be good if we could. It saves us having to jump through a few more hoops arranging permission to release them on state or federal land. Besides, Dakota and the cubs know your place. They're used to being in that part of the North Fork. I think they'd be comfortable there and have a better chance of staying around."

I pressed up against the grated opening atop the culvert and gave the prisoners inside a long look. Dakota met my stare with small, gentle eyes and a submissive countenance that reminded me more of black bears I had seen in captivity than of other grizz. Her gaze never hardened, never widened. She never tensed to make a move toward me or away. Nothing about her presence projected the least hint of intimidation.

In earlier years, the cubs would have been wearing new ear tags for future identification. Instead, they carried microchips, implanted under the skin behind their ears via a needle when they were sedated. The pair, which were brothers, stared at me with the same expression as their mother, gentle as you please, slightly worried, almost apologetic.

The last time I got this carried away anthropomorphizing, Stahr had lashed out and banged the part of the culvert between us so hard that it shocked me back to my senses. Dakota and the cubs just kept looking at me with eyes that I could not make myself interpret as anything other than beseeching. Here, I thought, were grizzlies that really could live in your yard without trouble. I felt like a kid getting attached to a stray. "Mom, they followed me home. Can we keep them?"

The rational part of my brain knew very well that I could stumble upon this mild-mannered trio one day and get torn apart for walking on my own North Fork property. But chance meetings with grizz had been part of life on the place since the day we bought it a quarter century before, including all the years we reared children there. If the odds with Dakota weren't as good as I wanted to believe, they were certainly no worse than with other bears. Either way, she wasn't going to keep to our small rectangle of land, not with the park across the river on our eastern boundary and national forest on the other three sides. Manley knew that. A release onto our place was in effect a release onto federal land but without the formalities.

"Sure," I told him. Within minutes, he had the pickup wound up and pointed to the North Fork, trailing the culvert packed with *horribilis* through miles of woodlands still smoldering from the massive wildfire until we passed out of the charred swath into green country again. We took them to the edge of our place, raised the trapdoor, and watched as three grizzly bears dashed out and onto the property, Dakota pausing only long enough to check on the cubs' progress behind her.

It was a satisfying moment, but it didn't do much good. While I went to hike on the east side of Glacier Park for a couple of days, the bear family was crossing the Whitefish Range back to the Stillwater Valley. By the time I got home, Dakota and her cubs had announced their return to everybody in Trego by parading through the yard of the small schoolhouse there.

Manley's colleague Tim Thier called to say that these grizzly antics were not making his life as the local wildlife biologist any easier and he would appreciate it if Manley could do something to cut down on the commotion. Manley arrived and dragged a road-killed deer to lay out a scent trail. It led to the far end of a pasture next to Thier's home. The biologists baited snares and a culvert trap there. When their quarry avoided them, Manley spent a day inside the culvert himself, using it as a shooter's blind. But his attempt to free-range Dakota was to no avail.

On the following day, September 27, Thier telephoned with the news that, from his vantage point, it looked as though both cubs were caught in snares, and Dakota was racing around by them. I hurried to Trego with Manley, then watched from a distance as he and Thier continued on to the trap site. Peering through my telescope, I could make out two snared grizz, but one of them was Dakota. It was a cub that was running loose.

The mother rose up frantic and raging, roaring, biting at the cable that held one front foot. She lifted the snared paw higher and pushed against the cable with her other front foot. Meanwhile, both cubs, the trapped one and its uncaught sibling, were whuffing and whining and raising dust from the dry duff on the forest floor. Dakota put her free paw on the noosed one and held both out before her, joined. While she was probably trying to claw the snare loose, it looked for all the world as though she was imploring us or fate or the Great Bear in the Sky to free her.

Manley and Thier shot the trapped grizzlies with darts. The other cub dashed away but soon returned and scuffled around its mother and brother, who were growing quiet as the immobilizing drug took effect. Manley darted that bear too. The little male fled uphill and started to climb a tree. Manley followed a ways and then simply waited. The cub returned, unable to keep apart, and collapsed next to the other bears. I helped lug all three into the culvert trap, backed up as close to the capture site as possible.

— — —

Carrie Hunt and her Wind River Bear Institute assistants had recently returned to Montana after a sojourn teaching bears in southern Alberta. At full strength again, the team had been busy in Olney, Trego, Fortine, and Stryker, going door-to-door to inform householders about the particular grizzlies in their neighborhood and how to avoid attracting them closer. Hunt and Manley gave talks at the local schools, including the one the bears had walked by. Most of the valley had heard about the grizzly family by now. No matter what their opinions on predators or conservation in general, folks found themselves following the fate of these three bears. They were becoming invested in grizz, if only by dint of normal curiosity.

Some wildlife professionals disapprove of naming study animals, feeling that it makes people less able to view species objectively. The point is well taken. Yet the public's overall level of concern goes up sharply when they feel they can identify with an individual creature—one that, like them, has a name, a certain temperament, and a personal history. The locals weren't interested in a generic grizz labeled No. 163. They wanted to hear the news on the mother bear from Dakota Avenue and those two cubs of hers.

The latest was that Manley, Hunt, and their crew had hauled the trio to the North Fork again—specifically, to my acreage. To help hold the bears there, the team placed a couple of deer carcasses on the property before the release. It worked. For a few days. Then the family wandered uphill a ways below Cyclone Peak, possibly because they were displaced by a larger female grizz with two yearling cubs that people reported seeing close to our place.

By mid-October, Dakota and her well-traveled offspring were down in the Stillwater Valley again. As before, they were highly visible around houses and on the railroad tracks. Yet they also kept to their pattern of ignoring bird seed and garbage in order to focus on natural foods—right up until they were discovered feeding on a dead cow in the center of a pasture near Fortine. When the rancher called the wildlife department, he naturally thought that the grizzlies might have killed his cow. Manley examined the remains, which Dakota had cached beneath a mound of clawed turf. He was able to tell that the cow had died long before the bears found it. Reassured, the rancher agreed to let the wildfire-displaced family stay and finish up the cow.

Dakota and the cubs had been bingeing on the carcass for ten days when, on October 26, Manley invited me along on a visit to the ranch. Carrie Hunt and her crew came too. With them was a tall, mustachioed, instantly likable cinematographer named Derek Reich. Reich used to work for major network news programs, frequently traveling abroad. He still filmed a variety of subjects on assignment. But since discovering *Ursus arctos horribilis,* their human instructors, and Karelian dogs, he had devoted months of his time to documenting this aspect of the grizzly recovery effort, helping the team out with ordinary chores and logistics in between.

Basically, Reich was doing the same sort of thing that I was, but putting more effort into it. He had no particular finished product or outlet in mind for his work, and neither did I. We were unrepentant grizz groupies—two guys with a serious silvertip-dependency problem and not the least interest in a cure. Reich was so hooked on the project that he had acquired his own Karelian, a robust male named Usko. On occasion, the dog rode in Reich's camper among the camping supplies, video cameras, and digital editing gear. More often, Usko traveled up front in the cab. The dog and I rode to the ranch jostling for space in the front seat.

The bear family was getting roly-poly on rotting steak in fairly secure surroundings, and life was fine. Accommodating as the rancher had been, though, he harbored a nagging fear that each day the grizzlies fed on beef made them more likely to go for the live variety. Besides that, he wanted to take off deer hunting for a while, and he didn't like the idea of grizz hanging around in his absence. Thus, our mission for the day was to drive them off the carcass and remove the leftovers for good.

Stopping in at the ranch house to let the owners know we were ready to proceed, Manley and Hunt found only the rancher's daughter-in-law at home. It was the first she had heard of the plan. "Aw, that's too bad," she said. "My dad's coming this weekend, and I wanted to show him Dakota." She told us to go ahead. As we drove into the pasture, luminous ground mist cut the visibility to a few dozen feet at times. Reich rolled his eyes, and we began a discussion of whether volunteering to snatch meat away from a grizzly in the fog meant that we were crazy or just not very bright.

Everyone was aware that grizzlies can be ornery as sin when confronted over a fresh kill or a carcass, but none of us seriously expected

Dakota to get testy. She wasn't the type. For that matter, she wasn't even there when we got close enough to see the cache. After holding off for some time, we hiked up a low rise through the woods to scout around. Dakota's signal told us that the family wasn't far away, but we couldn't spot anything in that direction. Taking advantage of their absence, we uncovered the cow, by now rendered into various ghoulish chunks, and dragged the stuff out with ropes to a small culvert trap, hauled behind one of the trucks to serve as a mobile refuse bin.

We dug for more than an hour through the enormous mound of dirt and pine needles that the bears had heaped together, making sure we got all the loose legs, segments of brisket, neck bones, and the like. I wouldn't expect television wildlife specials to dwell on such aspects of day-to-day grizzly bear management, any more than they would showcase the tedium of midnight stakeouts and schmoozing with local landowners. Nevertheless, the reporting ought to at least hint at the fact that every hour of observing the creatures is underpinned by fifty hours of poking apart turds, autopsying kills, packing around putrefying baits, swatting away flies, and so on.

Tunneling into one side of the bears' cache, I asked myself for the umpteenth time why, if working with grizzlies was so glamorous, I ended up stinking to high heaven half the days I went out with these people. I'd heard Manley describe his profession as "janitor extraordinaire" after sweeping up bird seed and packing livestock grain to secure quarters, but this was more like the grave-robbing business.

An hour after we dragged the last of the Halloween-ready corpse from the foot of the hill and withdrew, Dakota and the cubs appeared to the north of the site. Following a line of trees and streamside brush, they moseyed toward where the carcass had been, the cubs playing the entire time. As they reached their cache spot, Dakota detected the scent from our visit and stood up. The cubs stood as well, hurried to join mom, and the three trotted away together.

It was mid-afternoon before they returned, coming from the opposite direction this time. The cattle herd that had been farther out in the open pasture was now less than 200 feet from the bears.

Dakota ignored the cows but again caught an unsettling smell at the site and bolted. Familiar as she had to be with human-related odors after her many excursions through towns, a whiff where she wasn't expecting one could clearly still spook her.

Shortly thereafter, the grizzlies approached for a third time. The bear team was still waiting hundreds of yards downwind, patient as ever. They wanted the grizzlies to stay and inspect the ground sufficiently to grasp that their food supply was no longer there. Fifteen minutes later, around 5:00 P.M., the bears turned their backs on the site and ambled farther out into the pasture. A strong, cold wind had moved in from the west beneath a clear sky. At this stage of a Montana autumn, most of the golden leaves had fallen from the aspen and cottonwood branches. But the forests had been gilded a second time as the needles of western larch turned. Now the wind was plucking those loose along with the last offerings from a tall aspen stand, creating the effect of resplendent curtains falling slowly earthward behind the grizz. It was a scene of billowing grace, of untamed power within a framework of surpassing tranquility.

Or it was for a while; all at once, the team was driving toward the bears, yelling and shooting, letting the animals know that they were too far out in the open and no longer welcome in the vicinity. Dakota and the cubs fled. The team drew far back and resumed waiting in case a refresher lesson was in order. Around 6:15, with dusk beginning to gather, the grizzlies came over the crest of the hill, where the cattle had by then moved to graze. The bears passed among the cows almost like members of the herd and continued down into the big, open pasture. One of the cubs kept playing with Dakota every step of the way.

Where I had expected that the mother grizzly might be at least slightly grumpy about losing her regular meal, she was in a boisterous mood and romped with the little bear just as avidly as it pursued her. Dakota hopped in place. She made goof charges and somersaulted at the end of each run. The second cub joined in, and the play-wrestling escalated. More somersaulting ensued. You would have thought we were watching circus bears. Mom's enthusiasm didn't wane for a second. She stayed in full floppy mode, shimmying and shaking her head and waggling her rump, matching her youngsters bound for bound, slap for cuff.

After another somersault, she lay on her back and grabbed the base of her toes with the tips of her claws and rocked back and forth, a great, plump, furry seesaw. And that's really why I wanted to tell her story. Not for any episodes of high drama and hard breathing, but because of what occurred to me as I watched Dakota at that moment: Before we can say exactly what a grizzly bear is, much less what good it is, we first have to answer the question of why a fully grown, apex carnivore would retain this enormous capacity, this behavioral plasticity, this ineffable desire for fun.

Having sallied through the midst of live cattle to seek an old carcass, Dakota had joined in a prolonged bout of somersaulting and roughhousing with the two little bears who would follow her for at least one more year. In so doing, I thought she put to rest once and for all that one-dimensional representation of grizz as blood-lusty monsters. I thought that, as she held her toes and seesawed there, she called for a reconsideration of her kind.

Before darkness came, the bear team drove toward the grizzly family a final time. The crew took just one truck and made a slow approach, wishing only to remind Dakota "not to be so *visible*," as Carrie Hunt later said. Jumping up and down—I'd forgotten what Hunt's level of enthusiasm was like—she added, "That was exactly what we wanted to accomplish today. Dakota is such a good bear. But people are bothered by her, so we have to let her know that we want her to do a better job of keeping out of sight."

The next day, October 27, I drove to the Flathead County garbage dump and helped Manley unload the leftover cow from the culvert trap. He ended up crawling inside and pushing with his legs while I pulled on the slippery load from the outside. We wrestled it to the lip of the trap's door. But strain as we might, we couldn't budge the vile-smelling head and forequarters beyond that.

"What you got in there? Dead bear?" asked the guy dumping his pickup load of trash next to us. Most people in the valley recognized a culvert trap as a bear-catching device.

"Nah. Just an old cow."

"Grizzly kill it?"

"It died from something else and a grizzly got on it. We had to move it out of a pasture."

In the end, we ran a rope from the carcass to an immovable heap of junk and drove the trap out from under our gruesome load.

The man looked us over, noted the sweat, the clothes stained with the fluids of decomposition, looked again at the nearly formless heap of meat and hide at our feet, and declared, "I'm glad I don't have your job." He threw a few more items out of the pickup bed, glanced over again, and said with great sincerity, "I'll never complain about having to haul out old carpets again."

— — —

Earlier in the fall, a hunter bugling for bull elk—mimicking the call that males issue as a challenge to others—had attracted a grizzly that chewed up his leg. Then on October 30, a mother grizz with two older cubs killed a hunter at the southern edge of the Bob Marshall Wilderness. It happened after the man shot an elk. He had left the carcass in the field and gone to get supplies to butcher his kill and pack it out. During the interim, the grizzly family found the elk's body, fed on it, and partly buried it as their own meat cache. No one knows exactly what took place afterward except that the bears must have surprised the man upon his return.

It was the first death from a grizzly outside a national park in Montana since 1958, when a grizzly bear hunter was mauled to death by a male he had wounded. State and federal wildlife authorities moved in to the scene of the attack. They lured the grizzlies with bait and destroyed all three, and the event faded from the headlines.

Easy denned by the first week of November. Manley took it as a possible sign that she would emerge in the spring with her first litter of cubs, since pregnant grizzly females tend to hole up for the winter sooner than other females and emerge somewhat later. That same week, a homeowner shot a big male grizz near Eureka in the Tobacco Valley, north of the Stillwater, where Dakota lingered. The man said the bear, which had been breaking into a chicken coop, came toward him. This grizzly was missing a foot and was obviously having trouble feeding itself under natural conditions.

We followed Dakota west into the Salish Range and back toward Olney and then, finally, across Highway 93, which put her on the right side of the valley for a return to the Whitefish Range. One day, we went far up the side of Big Mountain and located Easy's signal emanating from her den. Dakota's frequency came in from downhill, closer to the valley floor than to the high, quiet places. In fact, she and the cubs were active not far from a meadow with houses and live-stock. Manley took an airplane flight and spotted the family after circling around their signal. "They look nice and round and healthy, even from the air," he told me. "Boy, I wish they would quit screwing around and just go hibernate."

It was the second week of December before he called to say that she and cubs had made it. They had denned almost a month late, but they were tucked inside the earth near the headwaters of a creek that drains east down the Whitefish Range to join the North Fork River near our property.

All three silvertipped bears were safe and in good condition, and that's the other reason I wanted to tell Dakota's story. Hers is a true tale of success. The odds were against her, but she and the bear team evened them out. Around the first week of April 2002, Manley made his first spring airplane flight. Easy was still snoozing, a further sign that she might emerge with young. Dakota and her cubs, now year-lings, were already out of the den. They weren't doing much yet. Manley saw them lying around not far from the den's entry and exit hole, as grizzlies tend to do for the first week or two out of hibernation. They were just taking it slow, gathering strength.

ODE TO BABYSITTERS

When traveling in Alaska several years ago, I read a newspaper report about a couple living in the bush near a salmon stream. One day as they looked up from their chores, they suddenly became aware that their daughter was no longer in sight. Slightly past the toddler stage, she had apparently wandered some distance from the cabin, for the parents heard no answer as they raced about calling her name. They widened their search but couldn't find her anywhere and feared she had fallen into the river.

After a while, she came skipping back home. They hugged her frantically and then demanded to know where she had been. "I was out playing with the bear family," she told them. Content to have her home safe, they probably laughed with relief at the imagination of children. Some time afterward, they walked along the river and found their daughter's footprints mixed with the tracks of a large grizzly and two smaller ones. From what they and local experts could read of the story in the sand, she had been playing with a bear family.

– – –

"A 16-month-old baby in Iran was found safe and slumbering in the den of a mother bear after being missing for three days. The *Kayhan* reported that the baby was the child of nomadic parents in western Lorestan province who found their child missing after returning to their tent from the fields. A search party later discovered the toddler in the bear's den about six miles from the encampment. The team said the child had been breast-fed by the bear, but doctors reported the baby was in good health. Other reports noted that brown bears in Iran are sometimes captured for use in entertainment in local bazaars as 'dancing bears.'"

—from *The Missoulian,*
a local Montana newspaper, October 8, 2001

EPILOGUE

IT'S LATE AUTUMN of 2002 as I write this. Tim Manley has now captured a total of seventy-three different grizzlies, many of them repeatedly, since 1993. He and Carrie Hunt performed aversive conditioning on a large percentage during the later years of that period. The team followed and tried to catch, or else succeeded in running off, dozens more. How many graduates of the bear education program are out there in the wild today would be impossible to say, since even those with radio collars drop them after a while and join the rest in obscurity.

My guess is that the group of alumni grizz remains a large one. I know it includes recent problem animals named Crystal and Sinclair. Their behavior improved during 2002, and Crystal, a young female, was seen in the company of a big male suitor. Of the bears met back in the tough year of 1998, Sully and the unnamed chicken thief from near Olney probably endure. Daryl and Blade, mere subadults when conditioned, could be roaming the Rockies for another twenty to twenty-five years. I hope that will somehow prove true as well for Speedo and Claire.

Stahr and her cubs still live on at the compound in Pullman, Washington, contributing information about the nutritional physiology of grizzlies simply by scarfing the food humans provide there.

In the spring of 2002, Easy once again came down from the upper rim of the Whitefish Range to graze on a mountainside golf course. People saw her on the twelfth green and in the yards of homes within that exclusive country club. The next reports put her four miles away, grazing in the yards of large, private estates at the head of Whitefish Lake. She was certainly working the upscale end of the human habitat spectrum. Contrary to Manley's expectations, none of the sightings mentioned cubs. He and Jay Honeyman, the Albertan who works for the Wind River Bear Institute, tracked Easy through those lawns and the surrounding woods daily. They never saw cubs either.

I went with them to get a fresh look at the bear. She appeared as golden and healthy as ever, staring back from among sprouting sedge and skunk cabbage by the mouth of a creek that feeds into the head of the lake. The marshy, verdant stream delta was the kind of place where grizzlies were supposed to come in early spring, and probably had since time immemorial. These days, it was too visible from a lakeshore road, and Easy was going too close to houses at night when she grazed the habitat converted to lawns.

Just as in other years, Manley and Honeyman yelled at Easy, fired cracker shells, and harassed her with dogs to encourage her to keep to thicker cover. Ideally, she would once again retreat up the mountainsides as the season progressed. But it was a slow, cold spring, even for Montana. Late snowstorms buried the new green growth more than once. Partway between the gated community's golf course and the lake's head, where Easy was roaming, a car struck and killed a grizzly cub on the lakeshore road. Later, another driver saw a cub trying to scramble up the steep road bank to get away. It kept sliding back. Even to an inexperienced eye, the infant seemed to lack vigor. The driver captured it and turned it over to the wildlife department. Which meant that the five-month-old grizzly ended up temporarily housed at Manley's.

My son, Russell, and I went over to see the cub. It was thin and undersized, scarcely larger than a housecat. It probably weighed less than eight pounds. The baby cowered motionless at the back of a plastic cage used for transporting dogs. Yet when Russell offered a bottle, it guzzled the formula without hesitation. The animal was starving and plainly had been for some time. There were two possible explanations, both cheerless. Either the mother of this little bear and its dead sibling had died while using the same general range as Easy, or the mother was Easy, in which case the cubs had become separated from her and never caught up. Easy had been seen alone for going on two weeks now.

Manley thought that it might be worth trying to reunite the cub with Easy. But because there was no definite proof that the two were related, and because Easy was in a questionable situation, pushing the limits of proximity to people, the cub went to the state wildlife department headquarters in Helena, Montana. Within several days, Manley and I were tracking Easy on the golf course again. Then she was back by the head of the lake, then up at some Big Mountain condos, then boldly looking for food down in the city of Whitefish. It was too much. The decision was made to take her out of circulation. Her capture, the sixth and final one, happened on the same street where another well-known female was originally caught: Dakota Avenue.

Easy was shipped to West Yellowstone, Montana, just outside Yellowstone National Park. She was not released into that ecosystem but into a pen at the Grizzly and Wolf Discovery Center, where bears otherwise slated for destruction live on public display. DNA samples confirmed that the orphan was her offspring. But the Discovery Center wasn't equipped for rearing cubs. The baby was sent on to the Denver Zoo instead. All the Montana bear crew had left of the family was endless speculation about how it got broken up in the first place.

Considering where Easy had spent time that spring, it wasn't difficult to envision a sudden encounter with people, automobiles, or neighborhood dogs causing the bears to race off in different directions and lose track of each other. Maybe Easy sent the cubs up a tree and then was spurred to continue fleeing. As a first-time mother, she may have lacked the skills or possibly even the level of attachment required to return and round up her babies. Whatever the case, two small future members of the Northern Continental Divide

Ecosystem grizzly bear population were gone, together with another slice of the reproductive potential embodied in breeding females such as their mother.

By autumn, a car had killed another grizzly, and a train creamed one more. A hunter mistook one for a black bear. Two silvertips were shot by people who felt threatened. Manley was called in to catch and euthanize an additional NCDE grizz, and a poacher left one from the beleaguered Cabinet-Yaak bear enclave to rot in the backwoods there. Those were just the deaths from Montana west of the Continental Divide—those that had been discovered, anyway.

East of the divide, several more grizzlies succumbed to the usual gamut of human causes, and a female with three cubs was shot in the head by a panicky hunter who had crawled up to within fifteen yards before realizing that the animal was neither a deer nor an elk. The mother bear lay half conscious for days, yet somehow managed to keep suckling the cubs. While I write, she is leading her young deeper into the mountains, staggering because one side is partially paralyzed. Everyone in the state is following this family's progress through news reports from the biologist tracking the bears. He says the mother's pace remains painfully slow, but she is becoming more and more mobile, improving by the day. In all, the year's toll has been no worse than most and much better than some.

As for Dakota, she and her offspring, now yearlings, basically repeated their itinerary of the previous year. With the exception of a side trip to the Stillwater Valley during June, the trio kept to the North Fork. They used habitats both inside Glacier Park and outside it, meandered through the bottomlands around Karen's and my place, and ascended toward Cyclone Peak with the onset of what turned into a fine berry season. Then, exactly as in 2001—minus the threat of wildfire—the family left the Whitefish Range for the Stillwater Valley. They passed a couple of weeks foraging here and there in the rural bottomlands and then found themselves some rotten beef.

It wasn't one cow this time but several that had died over summer. During early October, the bears disinterred them from a mass grave on the river's north bank. All things considered, this was as safe a spot as could be wished for in a settled valley. The rancher had no objection, and the bears could dig up cow parts, haul them straight downhill into riverside brush, and gorge away, hidden from view. Nobody lived in or frequented the immediate vicinity. The biggest threat came after word got out and grizzly aficionados arrived wanting to walk in from the road for close-up observations. After one self-proclaimed grizz expert was seen creeping riverward through the woods, the rancher made it clear that trespassing was forbidden.

I drove out to the ranch almost every day during the last half of October, usually with Manley. We would quickly scan the pastures and their cattle herds for bears, find none, locate Dakota's radio signal, then sit on the road's shoulder listening to it. Since the grizzlies were occasionally visible when they came up from the riverside to dig out the next gobbet of food, we often met other people waiting in their cars in hopes of a glimpse. Some of them got lucky. I never did. After two weeks of this, I accused Manley of secretly tossing a radio transmitter over the bank so he would have an excuse to come out to enjoy the sunrises and sunsets, watch deer in the fields and the coyotes and ravens by the boneyard, and yammer about grizz without ever having to actually work.

At the beginning of November, Dakota's signal moved north. She was leading the yearlings upriver through a mosaic of more cattle-filled pastures and new country homes. Manley answered a call from a man who reported that grizzlies had been in his garden after tearing through a fence. The tracks in the tilled soil and the claw marks he showed us on an apple tree were instantly recognizable as black bear sign. However, Manley took half an hour, hmmm-ing and ah-hah-ing and dropping hints, to let the homeowner, an avid hunter and outdoorsman, reach that conclusion himself. Face was saved. Grizz were exonerated. We moved on and pinpointed Dakota's signal along a brushy curve of the Stillwater.

The mother bear and yearlings slowly carried on north for a while, then turned east. The next time I went out with Manley

November 11, the handheld antenna pointed to a location away from the river's course and across Highway 93, the major barrier between these bears and the Whitefish Range. Following a logging road upslope, Manley almost casually pointed out the pickup window and said, "There she is. And there's one of the cubs."

They were among a clutter of stumps, brush, and conifer saplings in cutover land. I marveled that he had been able to spot either bear, especially while steering. He shrugged. "I knew from her signal that they had to be close," he told me. "Did you notice the way it started to get really blappy?" The answer was no. I had only spent hundreds of hours listening to the receiver go "Chweep, chweep, chweep." He had spent thousands. Picking out subtle differences in strength, including the type of reverberation (or "blap") that develops in close proximity, was second nature to him.

I had no more than a glance at the bears before they went out of view. It was enough to tell that Dakota was wide and wooly—wearing a splendid fall coat and plump as a hog. I could see how the tradition of calling male bears boars and females sows got started. The yearling in view stood almost as tall as Easy. "This is where they crossed the highway and started their move up into the mountains last year," Manley said. "I think they're on their way."

Over the days that followed, the bears gradually gained elevation in the Swift Creek drainage. Some loggers came upon their tracks. One man saw all three on the edge of the dirt road. On the 17th of November, Manley and Derek Reich, the cinematographer-turned-volunteer, located Dakota's signal so high up that they were sure the family was about to cross the snowy Whitefish Divide through the pass there. That would put the bears in the headwaters of the drainage where they had denned the previous year. I joined Manley and Reich on the 18th. The three grizz were still near the divide. Within the next forty-eight hours, they crossed over and into their winter rest area.

Dakota's offspring were big enough that they could leave their ~ther in 2003 to begin life on their own. If they do, Dakota could breed again and produce another set of cubs in 2004. And they in turn could commence the long, risky, amazing process of becoming a grown-up grizzly.

Is that how the real story of their lives will unfold? With grizz, the answer must be, as ever, Maybe. But I'd be willing to bet that Tim Manley will find out. I'll still be following the animals around too, watching them when I can. I no longer expect to fully understand the nature of grizzlies one day, or to grasp all that great bears mean to us in the modern world. The only things I feel fairly certain about are that every simplistic image of these fellow mammals, and every blanket solution for how to relate to them, reveals limitations on our part more than on theirs. And that while we may ultimately discover much of what we need to know through scientific data and logic, using our heads, the heart is sometimes a truer field guide.

A portion of the author's proceeds from this book
will go to Vital Ground, a small, nonprofit group that
safeguards habitat for grizzlies and other North American
wildlife through strategic land purchases and conservation
easements. For more information or to make a donation,
contact: Vital Ground, P.O. Box 982003,
Park City, UT 84098; 435-658-0009;
www.vitalground.org.